THE PENGUIN SHAKESPEARE
EDITED FROM THE ORIGINAL TEXT
BY G. B. HARRISON
B 3 I
CYMBELINE

WILLIAM SHAKESPEARE

The Tragedy of Cymbeline

PENGUIN BOOKS

Penguin Books Ltd, Harmondsworth, Middlesex
AUSTRALIA: Penguin Books Pty Ltd, 762 Whitehorse Road,
Mitcham, Victoria

—

This edition first published 1957

The Editor gratefully acknowledges
the kindness of Dr J. C. Adams in
allowing the Penguin Shakespeare to
reproduce an engraving of his
model of the stage of the
Globe Playhouse

The portraits on the cover and on the title page
were engraved by Reynolds Stone

—

Made and printed in Great Britain
by Wyman & Sons Ltd, London, Fakenham and Reading

CONTENTS

THE WORKS OF SHAKESPEARE

APPROXIMATE DATE	PLAYS	FIRST PRINTED
Before 1594	HENRY VI *three parts*	Folio 1623
	RICHARD III	1597
	TITUS ANDRONICUS	1594
	LOVE'S LABOUR'S LOST	1598
	THE TWO GENTLEMEN OF VERONA	Folio
	THE COMEDY OF ERRORS	Folio
	THE TAMING OF THE SHREW	Folio
1594–1597	ROMEO AND JULIET (*pirated* 1597)	1599
	A MIDSUMMER NIGHT'S DREAM	1600
	RICHARD II	1597
	KING JOHN	Folio
	THE MERCHANT OF VENICE	1600
1597–1600	HENRY IV *part i*	1598
	HENRY IV *part ii*	1600
	HENRY V (*pirated* 1600)	Folio
	MUCH ADO ABOUT NOTHING	1600
	MERRY WIVES OF WINDSOR (*pirated* 1602)	Folio
	AS YOU LIKE IT	Folio
	JULIUS CÆSAR	Folio
	TROYLUS AND CRESSIDA	1609
1601–1608	HAMLET (*pirated* 1603)	1604
	TWELFTH NIGHT	Folio
	MEASURE FOR MEASURE	Folio
	ALL'S WELL THAT ENDS WELL	Folio
	OTHELLO	1622
	LEAR	1608
	MACBETH	Folio
	TIMON OF ATHENS	Folio
	ANTONY AND CLEOPATRA	Folio
	CORIOLANUS	Folio
After 1608	PERICLES (*omitted from the Folio*)	1609
	CYMBELINE	Folio
	THE WINTER'S TALE	Folio
	THE TEMPEST	Folio
	HENRY VIII	Folio

POEMS

DATES UNKNOWN		
	VENUS AND ADONIS	1593
	THE RAPE OF LUCRECE	1594
	SONNETS }	1609
	A LOVER'S COMPLAINT }	
	THE PHŒNIX AND THE TURTLE	1601

WILLIAM SHAKESPEARE

William Shakespeare was born at Stratford upon Avon in April, 1564. He was the third child, and eldest son, of John Shakespeare and Mary Arden. His father was one of the most prosperous men of Stratford, who held in turn the chief offices in the town. His mother was of gentle birth, the daughter of Robert Arden of Wilmcote. In December, 1582, Shakespeare married Ann Hathaway, daughter of a farmer of Shottery, near Stratford; their first child Susanna was baptized on May 6, 1583, and twins, Hamnet and Judith, on February 22, 1585. Little is known of Shakespeare's early life; but it is unlikely that a writer who dramatized such an incomparable range and variety of human kinds and experiences should have spent his early manhood entirely in placid pursuits in a country town. There is one tradition, not universally accepted, that he fled from Stratford because he was in trouble for deer stealing, and had fallen foul of Sir Thomas Lucy, the local magnate; another that he was for some time a schoolmaster.

From 1592 onwards the records are much fuller. In March, 1592, the Lord Strange's players produced a new play at the Rose Theatre called *Harry the Sixth*, which was very successful, and was probably the *First Part of Henry VI*. In the autumn of 1592 Robert Greene, the best known of the professional writers, as he was dying wrote a letter to three fellow writers in which he warned them against the ingratitude of players in general, and in particular against an 'upstart crow' who 'supposes he is as much able to bombast out a blank verse as the best of you: and being an absolute Johannes Factotum is in his own conceit the only Shake-scene in a country'. This is the first reference to

Shakespeare, and the whole passage suggests that Shakespeare had become suddenly famous as a playwright. At this time Shakespeare was brought into touch with Edward Alleyne the great tragedian, and Christopher Marlowe, whose thundering parts of Tamburlaine, the Jew of Malta, and Dr Faustus Alleyne was acting, as well as Hieronimo, the hero of Kyd's *Spanish Tragedy*, the most famous of all Elizabethan plays.

In April, 1593, Shakespeare published his poem *Venus and Adonis,* which was dedicated to the young Earl of Southampton: it was a great and lasting success, and was reprinted nine times in the next few years. In May, 1594, his second poem, *The Rape of Lucrece,* was also dedicated to Southampton.

There was little playing in 1593, for the theatres were shut during a severe outbreak of the plague; but in the autumn of 1594, when the plague ceased, the playing companies were reorganized, and Shakespeare became a sharer in the Lord Chamberlain's company who went to play in the Theatre in Shoreditch. During these months Marlowe and Kyd had died. Shakespeare was thus for a time without a rival. He had already written the three parts of *Henry VI, Richard III, Titus Andronicus, The Two Gentlemen of Verona, Love's Labour's Lost, The Comedy of Errors,* and *The Taming of the Shrew.* Soon afterwards he wrote the first of his greater plays – *Romeo and Juliet* – and he followed this success in the next three years with *A Midsummer Night's Dream, Richard II,* and *The Merchant of Venice.* The two parts of *Henry IV,* introducing Falstaff, the most popular of all his comic characters, were written in 1597–8.

The company left the Theatre in 1597 owing to disputes over a renewal of the ground lease, and went to play at the Curtain in the same neighbourhood. The disputes continued throughout 1598, and at Christmas the players settled the matter by demolishing the old Theatre and re-erecting a new playhouse on the South bank of the Thames, near Southwark Cathedral. This playhouse was named the Globe. The expenses of the new building were shared by the chief members of the Company, including Shakespeare, who was now a man of some means. In 1596 he had bought New Place, a large house in the centre of Stratford, for £60, and through his father purchased a coat-of-arms from the Heralds, which was the official recognition that he and his family were gentlefolk.

By the summer of 1598 Shakespeare was recognized as the greatest of English dramatists. Booksellers were printing his more popular plays, at times even in pirated or stolen versions, and he received a remarkable tribute from a young writer named Francis Meres, in his book *Palladis Tamia*. In a long catalogue of English authors Meres gave Shakespeare more prominence than any other writer, and mentioned by name twelve of his plays.

Shortly before the Globe was opened, Shakespeare had completed the cycle of plays dealing with the whole story of the Wars of the Roses with *Henry V*. It was followed by *As You Like It,* and *Julius Caesar,* the first of the maturer tragedies. In the next three years he wrote *Troylus and Cressida, The Merry Wives of Windsor, Hamlet,* and *Twelfth Night*.

On March 24, 1603, Queen Elizabeth I died. The company had often performed before her, but they found her successor a far more enthusiastic patron. One of the first acts of King James was to take over the company and to promote them to be his own servants, so that henceforward they were known as the King's Men. They acted now very frequently at Court, and prospered accordingly. In the early years of the reign Shakespeare wrote the more sombre comedies, *All's Well that Ends Well,* and *Measure for Measure,* which were followed by *Othello, Macbeth,* and *King Lear*. Then he returned to Roman themes with *Antony and Cleopatra* and *Coriolanus*.

Since 1601 Shakespeare had been writing less, and there were now a number of rival dramatists who were introducing new styles of drama, particularly Ben Jonson (whose first successful comedy, *Every Man in his Humour,* was acted by Shakespeare's company in 1598), Chapman, Dekker, Marston, and Beaumont and Fletcher who began to write in 1607. In 1608 the King's Men acquired a second playhouse, an indoor private theatre in the fashionable quarter of the Blackfriars. At private theatres, plays were performed indoors; the prices charged were higher than in the public playhouses, and the audience consequently was more select. Shakespeare seems to have retired from the stage about this time: his name does not occur in the various lists of players after 1607. Henceforward he lived for the most part at Stratford, where he was regarded as one of the most important citizens. He still wrote a few plays, and he tried his hand at the new form of tragi-comedy – a play with tragic incidents but a happy ending – which Beaumont and Fletcher had popularized. He wrote four of these – *Pericles, Cymbeline, The Winter's Tale,* and *The Tempest,* which was acted at Court in 1611. For the last four years of his life he lived in retirement. His son Hamnet had died in 1596: his two daughters were now married. Shakespeare died at Stratford upon Avon on April 23, 1616, and was buried in the chancel of the church, before the high altar. Shortly afterwards a memorial which still exists, with a portrait bust, was set up on the North wall. His wife survived him.

When Shakespeare died fourteen of his plays had been separately published in Quarto booklets. In 1623 his surviving fellow actors, John Heming and Henry Condell, with the co-operation of a number of printers, published a collected edition of thirty-six plays in one Folio volume, with an engraved portrait, memorial verses by Ben Jonson and others, and an Epistle to the Reader in which Heming and Condell make the interesting note that Shakespeare's 'hand and mind went together, and what he thought, he uttered with that easiness that we have scarce received from him a blot in his papers'.

The plays as printed in the Quartos or the Folio differ considerably from the usual modern text. They are often not divided into scenes, and sometimes not even into acts. Nor are there place-headings at the beginning of each scene, because in the Elizabethan theatre there was no scenery. They are carelessly printed and the spelling is erratic.

THE ELIZABETHAN THEATRE

Although plays of one sort and another had been acted for many generations, no permanent playhouse was erected in England until 1576. In the 1570s the Lord Mayor and Aldermen of the City of London and the players were constantly at variance. As a result James Burbage, then the leader of the great Earl of Leicester's players, decided that he would erect a playhouse outside the jurisdiction of the Lord Mayor, where the players would no longer be hindered by the authorities. Accordingly in 1576 he built the Theatre in Shoreditch, at that time a suburb of London. The experiment was successful, and by 1592 there were two more playhouses in London, the Curtain (also in Shoreditch), and the Rose on the south bank of the river, near Southwark Cathedral.

Elizabethan players were accustomed to act on a variety of stages; in the great hall of a nobleman's house, or one of the Queen's palaces, in town halls and in yards, as well as their own theatre.

The public playhouse for which most of Shakespeare's plays were written was a small and intimate affair. The outside measurement of the Fortune Theatre, which was built in 1600 to rival the new Globe, was but eighty feet square. Playhouses were usually circular or octagonal, with three tiers of galleries looking down upon the yard or pit, which was open to the sky. The stage jutted out into the yard so that the actors came forward into the midst of their audience.

Over the stage there was a roof, and on either side doors by which the characters entered or disappeared. Over the back of the stage ran a gallery or upper stage, with windows on either side, which was used whenever an upper scene was needed, as when Romeo climbs up to Juliet's bedroom, or the citizens of Angiers address King John from the walls. The space beneath this upper stage was known as the tiring house; it was concealed from the audience by a curtain which would be drawn back to reveal an inner stage, for such scenes as the witches' cave in *Macbeth*, Prospero's cell, or Juliet's tomb.

There was no general curtain concealing the whole stage, so that all scenes on the main stage began with an entrance and ended with an exit. Thus in tragedies the dead must be carried away. There was no scenery, and therefore no limit to the number of scenes, for a scene came to an end when the characters left the stage. When it was necessary for the exact locality of a scene to be known, then Shakespeare indicated it in the dialogue; otherwise a simple property or a garment was sufficient; a chair or stool showed an indoor scene, a man wearing riding boots was a messenger, a king wearing armour was on the battlefield, or the like. Such simplicity was on the whole an advantage; the spectator was not distracted by the setting and Shakespeare was able to use as many scenes as he wished. The action passed by very quickly: a play of 2500 lines of verse could be acted in two hours. Moreover, since the actor was so close to his audience, the slightest subtlety of voice and gesture was easily appreciated.

THE GLOBE THEATRE
Wood–engraving by R. J. Beedham after a reconstruction by J. C. Adams

The company was a 'Fellowship of Players', who were all partners and sharers. There were usually ten to fifteen full members, with three or four boys, and some paid servants. Shakespeare had therefore to write for his team. The chief actor in the company was Richard Burbage, who first distinguished himself as Richard III; for him Shakespeare wrote his great tragic parts. An important member of the company was the clown or low comedian. From 1594 to 1600 the company's clown was Will Kemp; he was succeeded by Robert Armin. No women were allowed to appear on the stage, and all women's parts were taken by boys.

CYMBELINE

Cymbeline was probably written in 1610. It was among those plays being acted in London in the early months of 1611 that were seen and summarized by Dr Simon Forman. In Forman's notebook the date of the performance is not recorded, but *Cymbeline* comes between a notice of *Macbeth*, seen on 20 April 1611, and a play on Richard II, seen on 30 April. Forman's account reads: *

'Of Cimbalin king of England.

'Remember also the storri of Cymbalin king of England, in Lucius tyme, howe Lucius Cam from Octauus Cesar for Tribut, and being denied, after sent Lucius with a greate Arme of Souldiars who landed at Milford hauen, and Affter wer vanquished by Cimbalin, and Lucius taken prisoner, and all by means of 3 outlawes, of the which 2 of them were the sonns of Cimbalim, stolen from him when they were but 2 yers old by an old man whom Cymbalin banished, and he kept them as his own sonns 20 yers with him in A cave. And howe (one) of them slewe Clotan, that was the quens sonn, goinge to Milford hauen to sek the loue of Innogen the kinges daughter, whom he had banished also for louinge his daughter, and howe the Italian that cam from her loue conveied him selfe into A Cheste, and said yt was a chest of plate sent from her loue & others, to be presented to the kinge. And in the depest of the night, she being aslepe, he opened the cheste, & cam forth of yt, And vewed her in her bed, and the markes of her body, & toke awai her braslet, & after Accused her of adultery to her loue, &c. And in thend howe he came with

* E. K. Chambers, *William Shakespeare*, Vol. II, pp. 338–9.

the Romains into England & was taken prisoner, and after
Reueled to Innogen, Who had turned her self into mans
apparrell & fled to mete her loue at Milford hauen, &
chanchsed to fall on the Caue in the wodes where her 2
brothers were, & howe by eating a sleping Dram they
thought she had bin deed, & laid her in the wodes, & the
body of Cloten by her, in her loues apparrell that he left
behind him, & howe she was found by Lucius, &c.'

Apart from this account, there is no other direct evidence for the date of writing, though the style shows that
Cymbeline was written in Shakespeare's latest period.

The historical scenes, which tell how Cymbeline, King
of Britain – for the story is supposed to take place in the
first century B.C. – had trouble with the Romans, came in
part from Holinshed's *Chronicles,* so often used by Shakespeare. But Shakespeare's use of the *Chronicles* in writing
Cymbeline was very different from his debt in the *Henry
IV* and *Henry V* plays, where he followed the narrative
closely. In Holinshed's account of Cymbeline there was
less material for drama, for in the early pages of the
Chronicles Holinshed was usually brief (and wholly un-
reliable) in his picturesque fables of the kings of Britain in
pre-Saxon days.

According to Holinshed –

'Kymbeline or Cimbeline, the son of Theomantius, was
of the Britons made king after the decease of his father, in
the year of the world 3944, after the building of Rome
728, and before the birth of our Saviour 33. This man (as
some write) was brought up at Rome, and there made
knight by Augustus Caesar, under whom he served in the
wars, and was in such favour with him, that he was at
liberty to pay his tribute or not.'

The episode of the fight in the narrow lane (P. 113

L. 6, P. 114 L. 18) was also taken from Holinshed – but from an incident in Scottish history which occurred nearly a thousand years after the reign of Cymbeline, when the Scots king was fighting Danish invaders:

'[The Danes] rushed forth with such violence upon their adversaries, that first the right, and then after the left wing of the Scots, was constrained to retire and flee back, the middle ward stoutly yet keeping their ground: but the same stood in such danger, being now left naked on the sides, that the victory must needs have remained with the Danes, had not a renewer of the battle come in time, by the appointment (as is to be thought) of Almighty God.

'For as it chanced, there was in the next field at the same time an husbandman, with two of his sons busy about his work, named Hay, a man strong and stiff in making and shape of body, but endued with a valiant courage. This Hay beholding the king with the most part of the nobles, fighting with great valiancy in the middle ward, now destitute of the wings, and in great danger to be oppressed by the great violence of his enemies, caught a plow beam in his hand, and with the same exhorting his sons to do the like, hasted toward the battle, there to die rather amongst others in defense of his country, than to remain alive after the discomfiture in miserable thralldom and bondage of the cruel and most unmerciful enemies. There was near to the place of the battle, a long lane fenced on the sides with ditches and walls made of turf, through the which the Scots which fled were beaten down by the enemies on heaps.

'Here Hay with his sons, supposing they might best stay the flight, placed themselves overthwart the lane, beat them back whom they met fleeing, and spared neither friend nor foe: but down they went all such as came within their reach, wherewith divers hardy personages cried unto their fellows to return back unto the battle, for there was a new power of Scottishmen come to their succours, by whose aid the victory might be easily obtained of their most cruel adversaries the Danes: therefore might they choose whether they would be slain of their own fellows coming to their aid, or to return again to fight with the enemies. The Danes being here stayed in the lane by the great valiancy of the father and the sons, thought verily there had been some great succours of Scots come to the aid of their king, and thereupon ceasing from further pursuit, fled back in great disorder unto the other of their fellows fighting with the middle ward of the Scots.'

The story of Imogen, Posthumus, and Iachimo was derived from a tale in Boccaccio's *Decameron* (Second Day, Ninth Tale), which may be summarized as follows:

Certain Italian merchants, gathered in Paris, after a jolly evening began to tell stories about their wives of whose loyalty they had a low opinion. But one of them, a Genoese called Bernarbo Lomellin, declared that he had a perfect wife and that it would be impossible to find a woman more chaste. Among the merchants was a young man called Ambrogiuolo da Piacenza, who began to mock Bernarbo, and to declare that if he had access to the lady, he would soon have the same success with her as with every other woman that he had encountered. At this, Bernarbo grew so angry that he was willing to wager his own head against one thousand crowns that Ambrogiulo would not succeed in his attempt. However, the wager ultimately fixed was that Bernarbo would pay five thousand florins if Ambrogiuolo succeeded, and win one thousand if he failed.

Ambrogiuolo set out for Genoa, where he made careful inquiries and soon learned that the lady was indeed as good as her husband had boasted. Realizing that his design was hopeless and being unwilling to lose his money, Ambrogiuolo bribed a poor woman who worked in the house to convey him in a chest into the lady's bedroom. Late that night, Ambrogiuolo opened the chest and stepped out; and since there was a light in the room he was able to note the pictures and other details. Then he approached the bed and uncovered the lady, perceiving under her left breast a mole surrounded with golden hairs. He also took from the lady's boxes, a purse, a gown, a ring, and a girdle, and so returned into the chest.

Ambrogiuolo hastened back to Paris with his trophies and claimed that he had won the wager. When he described the room and produced the articles he had stolen, Bernarbo acknowledged the accuracy of his tale but declared that he might have come by the tokens through one of the servants, and that better evidence was needed to win the bet. To this Ambrogiuolo retorted, 'This should be enough; but since you require something further, I will satisfy you. I say that the Lady Zinevra, your wife, has a mole under her left breast, around which are about six golden hairs.'

When Bernarbo heard these words he was struck to the heart and admitted that Ambrogiuolo had indeed won the wager. On the next day, having paid his bet, Bernarbo set out for Genoa. He did not go home but stayed at one of his estates about twenty miles outside the city. From here he sent one of his servants with a letter to his wife telling her to come out and meet him; but he ordered the servant to slay her on the way. The lady was very glad to receive the letter, and next day rode forth with the servant to meet her husband. When they came to a deep and lonely gorge, the servant drew a knife and was about to slay his mistress; but she pleaded with him so hard that he consented to give her some of his clothes and to take hers to Bernarbo with the tale that she was dead. Bernarbo thereafter returned to

Genoa, where he was much blamed for this supposed cruelty.

Meanwhile the poor lady, disguised as a man, made her way to the seacoast where she was taken into service by a Catalan gentleman called Signor Encararch. She now took the name of Sicurano da Finale. Sometime later the Catalan gentleman sailed to Alexandria, where the Soldan [Sultan] was so much attracted by the good service of Sicurano that he begged the Catalan for him. Sicurano quickly rose in the favour of the Soldan and was sent to Acre as governor and captain of the guard for the protection of the merchants there. Now, it so happened that Sicurano, as 'he' was looking into a shop belonging to a Venetian, saw the very purse and girdle that had been stolen by Ambrogiuolo. He asked the shopkeeper, who was Ambrogiuolo himself, how he had come by these articles. Ambrogiuolo replied that they had been given to him by a lady named Zinevra, wife of Bernarbo Lomellin, with whom he had spent the night; she had prayed him to keep them as a token of her love. In consequence, he had won a bet from Bernarbo, and Bernarbo had had Zinevra put to death.

Sicurano thus realized why her husband had treated her so cruelly. On returning to Alexandria, she caused the Soldan to be interested in Ambrogiuolo, and by a device she also caused Bernarbo to come to Alexandria. In the presence of the Soldan, Ambrogiuolo confessed the truth.

Then Sicurano, turning to the Soldan, said that she would produce the lady if the Soldan would punish the evildoers. The Soldan agreed. At this Sicurano, bursting into tears, cried out that she was the unfortunate Lady Zinevra, and rending her robes made it clear to the Sultan that she was in fact a woman. Bernarbo was forgiven for his cruelty and restored to his lady who was highly favoured by the Sultan; but Ambrogiuolo was bound to a stake and left with his bare flesh anointed with honey to be eaten away by the flies and wasps of that country.

As a whole *Cymbeline* has many resemblances to Beaumont and Fletcher's *Philaster*, which also concerns the misfortunes of a faithful lady, who owing to hasty misunderstanding is scorned, maligned, and ill-treated by her true-love. If, as is likely, *Philaster* was the earlier play, Shakespeare was following rather than creating a new vogue for tragi-comedy.

Cymbeline was first printed in the first Folio of 1623, where it is the last play in the volume; there was no previous Quarto. The original text was carefully prepared and there are few difficulties. The scribe who was responsible for the copy marked the divisions into Acts and Scenes; he had a good feeling for dramatic punctuation but he had also an excessive fondness for the use of capital letters. In this edition, in accordance with the principles adapted for the Penguin Shakespeares, the Folio has been followed closely: spellings have been conservatively modernized, the excess of capitals has been somewhat abated, but the orginal punctuation has been kept, except in a few instances where it seemed obviously wrong.

The Tragedy of
Cymbeline

THE ACTORS' NAMES

CYMBELINE, King of Britain
CLOTEN, the King's stepson, son of his Queen
POSTHUMUS LEONATUS, a gentleman
BELARIUS, a banished Lord, alias Morgan
GUIDERIUS } sons to Cymbeline, stolen in infancy, alias
ARVIRAGUS } Polydore and Cadwall
PHILARIO, friend to Posthumus, an Italian
IACHIMO, an Italian
CAIUS LUCIUS, the Roman Ambassador
PISANIO, servant to Posthumus
CORNELIUS, a physician
A ROMAN CAPTAIN
TWO BRITISH CAPTAINS
A FRENCH GENTLEMAN
LORDS
GENTLEMEN
JAILERS
THE QUEEN, Cymbeline's wife, mother to Cloten
IMOGEN, Cymbeline's daughter
A LADY ATTENDING ON IMOGEN
A SOOTHSAYER
Other Lords and Attendants and Soldiers
Ghosts of Posthumus's Father, Mother and Brothers

I. 1

Enter two Gentlemen.

1 GENTLEMAN: You do not meet a man but frowns.
Our bloods no more obey the Heavens
Than our Courtiers:
Still seem, as does the King's.

2 GENTLEMAN: But what's the matter?

1 GENTLEMAN: His daughter, and the heir of's kingdom
(whom
He purpos'd to his wife's sole Son, a Widow
That late he married) hath referr'd herself
Unto a poor, but worthy Gentleman. She's wedded,
Her Husband banish'd: she imprison'd, all
Is outward sorrow, though I think the King
Be touch'd at very heart.

2 GENTLEMAN: None but the King?

1 GENTLEMAN: He that hath lost her too: so is the Queen,
That most desir'd the match. But not a Courtier,
Although they wear their faces to the bent
Of the King's looks, hath a heart that is not
Glad at the thing they scowl at.

2 GENTLEMAN: And why so?

1 GENTLEMAN: He that hath miss'd the Princess, is a thing
Too bad, for bad report: and he that hath her,
(I mean, that married her, alack good man,
And therefore banish'd) is a creature, such,
As to seek through the Regions of the Earth
For one, his like; there would be something failing
In him, that should compare. I do not think,
So fair an outward, and such stuff within
Endows a man, but he.

2 GENTLEMAN: You speak him far.

1 GENTLEMAN: I do extend him (Sir) within himself,

Crush him together, rather than unfold
His measure duly.

2 GENTLEMAN: What's his name, and birth?

1 GENTLEMAN: I cannot delve him to the root: His
 Father
Was call'd Sicillius, who did join his honour
Against the Romans, with Cassibulan,
But had his titles by Tenantius, whom
He serv'd with glory, and admir'd success:
So gain'd the sur-addition, Leonatus.
And had (besides this Gentleman in question)
Two other Sons, who in the wars o'th'time
Died with their swords in hand. For which, their Father
Then old, and fond of issue, took such sorrow
That he quit being; and his gentle Lady
Big of this Gentleman (our theme) deceas'd
As he was born. The King he takes the babe
To his protection, calls him Posthumus Leonatus,
Breeds him, and makes him of his Bedchamber,
Puts to him all the learnings that his time
Could make him the receiver of, which he took
As we do air, fast as 'twas minister'd,
And in's spring, became a harvest: Liv'd in Court
(Which rare it is to do) most prais'd, most lov'd,
A sample to the youngest: to th'more mature,
A glass that feated them: and to the graver,
A child that guided dotards. To his Mistress,
(For whom he now is banish'd) her own price
Proclaims how she esteem'd him; and his virtue
By her election may be truly read, what kind of man he is.

2 GENTLEMAN: I honour him, even out of your report.
But pray you tell me, is she sole child to'th'King?

1 GENTLEMAN: His only child:
He had two Sons (if this be worth your hearing,
Mark it) the eldest of them, at three years old

I'th'swathing clothes, the other from their nursery
Were stolen, and to this hour, no guess in knowledge
Which way they went.

2 GENTLEMAN: How long is this ago?

I GENTLEMAN: Some twenty years.

2 GENTLEMAN: That a King's children should be so
  convey'd,
So slackly guarded, and the search so slow
That could not trace them.

I GENTLEMAN: Howsoe'er, 'tis strange,
Or that the negligence may well be laugh'd at:
Yet is it true Sir.

2 GENTLEMAN: I do well believe you.

I GENTLEMAN: We must forbear. Here comes the
  Gentleman,
The Queen, and Princess.
                              Exeunt.

I.2

Enter the Queen, Posthumus, and Imogen.

QUEEN: No, be assur'd you shall not find me (Daughter)
After the slander of most Step-Mothers,
Evil-ey'd unto you. You're my prisoner, but
Your jailer shall deliver you the keys
That lock up your restraint. For you Posthumus,
So soon as I can win th'offended King,
I will be known your advocate: marry yet
The fire of rage is in him, and 'twere good
You lean'd unto his sentence, with what patience
Your wisdom may inform you.

POSTHUMUS: 'Please your Highness,
I will from hence today.

QUEEN: You know the peril:
I'll fetch a turn about the Garden, pitying

The pangs of barr'd affections, though the King
Hath charg'd you should not speak together.

Exit.

IMOGEN: O dissembling courtesy! How fine this Tyrant
Can tickle where she wounds? My dearest Husband,
I something fear my Father's wrath, but nothing
(Always reserv'd my holy duty) what
His rage can do on me. You must be gone,
And I shall here abide the hourly shot
Of angry eyes: not comforted to live,
But that there is this Jewel in the world,
That I may see again.

POSTHUMUS: My Queen, my Mistress:
O Lady, weep no more, least I give cause
To be suspected of more tenderness
Than doth become a man. I will remain
The loyal'st husband, that did ere plight troth.
My residence in Rome, at one Philario's,
Who, to my Father was a friend, to me
Known but by letter; thither write (my Queen)
And with mine eyes, I'll drink the words you send,
Though ink be made of gall.

Enter Queen.

QUEEN: Be brief, I pray you:
If the King come, I shall incur, I know not
How much of his displeasure: yet I'll move him
To walk this way: I never do him wrong,
But he does buy my injuries, to be friends:
Pays dear for my offences.

POSTHUMUS: Should we be taking leave
As long a term as yet we have to live,
The loathness to depart, would grow: Adieu.

IMOGEN: Nay, stay a little:
Were you but riding forth to air yourself,
Such parting were too petty. Look here (Love)

This diamond was my Mother's; take it (Heart)
But keep it till you woo another Wife,
When Imogen is dead.

POSTHUMUS: How, how? Another?
You gentle Gods, give me but this I have,
And sear up my embracements from a next,
With bonds of death. Remain, remain thou here,
While sense can keep it on: And sweetest, fairest,
As I (my poor self) did exchange for you
To your so infinite loss; so in our trifles
I still win of you. For my sake wear this,
It is a manacle of Love, I'll place it
Upon this fairest Prisoner.

IMOGEN: O the Gods!
When shall we see again?

Enter Cymbeline, and Lords.

POSTHUMUS: Alack, the King.

CYMBELINE: Thou basest thing, avoid hence, from my
    sight;
If after this command thou fraught the Court
With thy unworthiness, thou diest. Away,
Thou'rt poison to my blood.

POSTHUMUS: The Gods protect you,
And bless the good remainders of the Court:
I am gone.

Exit.

IMOGEN: There cannot be a pinch in death
More sharp than this is.

CYMBELINE: O disloyal thing,
That should'st repair my youth, thou heap'st
A year's age on me.

IMOGEN: I beseech you Sir,
Harm not yourself with your vexation,
I am senseless of your wrath; a touch more rare
Subdues all pangs, all fears.

CYMBELINE: Past grace? Obedience?

IMOGEN: Past hope, and in despair, that way past grace.

CYMBELINE: That might'st have had
The sole Son of my Queen.

IMOGEN: O blessed, that I might not: I chose an Eagle,
And did avoid a Puttock.

CYMBELINE: Thou took'st a Beggar, would'st have made
my Throne, a seat for baseness.

IMOGEN: No, I rather added a lustre to it.

CYMBELINE: O thou vile one!

IMOGEN: Sir,
It is your fault that I have lov'd Posthumus:
You bred him as my play-fellow, and he is
A man, worth any woman: Over-buys me
Almost the sum he pays.

CYMBELINE: What? art thou mad?

IMOGEN: Almost Sir: Heaven restore me: would I were
A neat-herd's daughter, and my Leonatus
Our neighbour-shepherd's Son.

Enter Queen.

CYMBELINE: Thou foolish thing;
They were again together: you have done
Not after our command. Away with her,
And pen her up.

QUEEN: Beseech your patience: Peace
Dear Lady daughter, peace. Sweet Sovereign,
Leave us to ourselves, and make yourself some comfort
Out of your best advice.

CYMBELINE: Nay, let her languish
A drop of blood a day, and being aged
Die of this folly.

Exit.
Enter Pisanio.

QUEEN: Fie, you must give way:
Here is your Servant. How now Sir? What news?

PISANIO: My Lord your son, drew on my Master.
QUEEN: Hah?
  No harm I trust is done?
PISANIO: There might have been,
  But that my Master rather played, than fought,
  And had no help of Anger: they were parted
  By Gentlemen, at hand.
QUEEN: I am very glad on't.
IMOGEN: Your Son's my Father's friend, he takes his part
  To draw upon an exile. O brave Sir,
  I would they were in Africk both together,
  Myself by with a needle, that I might prick
  The goer back. Why came you from your Master?
PISANIO: On his command: he would not suffer me
  To bring him to the Haven: left these notes
  Of what commands I should be subject to,
  When't pleas'd you to employ me.
QUEEN: This hath been
  Your faithful Servant: I dare lay mine honour
  He will remain so.
PISANIO: I humbly thank your Highness.
QUEEN: Pray walk awhile.
IMOGEN: About some half hour hence,
  Pray you speak with me;
  You shall (at least) go see my Lord aboard.
  For this time leave me.
                    Exeunt.

I.3 [I.2]

Enter Cloten, and two Lords.

1 LORD: Sir, I would advise you to shift a shirt; the
  violence of action hath made you reek as a sacrifice:
  where air comes out, air comes in: There's none abroad
  so wholesome as that you vent.

CLOTEN: If my shirt were bloody, then to shift it.
Have I hurt him?

2 LORD: No faith: not so much as his patience.

1 LORD: Hurt him? His body's a passable carcase if he be
not hurt. It is a through-fare for steel if it be not hurt.

2 LORD: His steel was in debt, it went o'th'backside the
Town.

CLOTEN: The Villain would not stand me.

2 LORD: No, but he fled forward still, toward your face.

1 LORD: Stand you? you have land enough of your own:
But he added to your having, gave you some ground.

2 LORD: As many inches, as you have oceans (Puppies.)

CLOTEN: I would they had not come between us.

2 LORD: So would I, till you had measur'd how long a
Fool you were upon the ground.

CLOTEN: And that she should love this Fellow, and refuse
me.

2 LORD: If it be a sin to make a true election, she is
damn'd.

1 LORD: Sir, as I told you always: her beauty and her
brain go not together. She's a good sign, but I have seen
small reflection of her wit.

2 LORD: She shines not upon fools, lest the reflection
Should hurt her.

CLOTEN: Come, I'll to my chamber: would there had
been some hurt done.

2 LORD: I wish not so, unless it had been the fall of an Ass,
which is no great hurt.

CLOTEN: You'll go with us?

1 LORD: I'll attend your Lordship.

CLOTEN: Nay come, let's go together.

2 LORD: Well my Lord.

Exeunt.

I.4 [I.3]

Enter Imogen and Pisanio.

IMOGEN: I would thou grew'st unto the shores o'th'
  Haven
  And questioned'st every sail: if he should write,
  And I not have it, 'twere a paper lost
  As offer'd mercy is: What was the last
  That he spake to thee?

PISANIO: It was his Queen, his Queen.

IMOGEN: Then wav'd his handkerchief?

PISANIO: And kiss'd it, Madam.

IMOGEN: Senseless linen, happier therein than I:
  And that was all?

PISANIO: No Madam: for so long
  As he could make me with his eye, or ear,
  Distinguish him from others, he did keep
  The deck, with glove, or hat, or handkerchief,
  Still waving, as the fits and stirs of 's mind
  Could best express how slow his soul sail'd on,
  How swift his ship.

IMOGEN: Thou should'st have made him,
  As little as a crow, or less, ere left
  To after-eye him.

PISANIO: Madam, so I did.

IMOGEN: I would have broke mine eye-strings;
  Crack'd them, but to look upon him, till the diminution
  Of space, had pointed him sharp as my needle:
  Nay, followed him, till he had melted from
  The smallness of a gnat, to air: and then
  Have turn'd mine eye, and wept. But good Pisanio,
  When shall we hear from him.

PISANIO: Be assur'd Madam,
  With his next vantage.

B

IMOGEN: I did not take my leave of him, but had
    Most pretty things to say: Ere I could tell him
    How I would think on him at certain hours,
    Such thoughts, and such: Or I could make him swear,
    The She's of Italy should not betray
    Mine interest, and his honour: or have charg'd him
    At the fix'd hour of morn, at noon, at midnight,
    T'encounter me with orisons, for then
    I am in Heaven for him: Or ere I could,
    Give him that parting kiss, which I had set
    Betwixt two charming words, comes in my Father,
    And like the tyrannous breathing of the North,
    Shakes all our buds from growing.

                        Enter a Lady.

LADY: The Queen (Madam)
    Desires your Highness' company.

IMOGEN: Those things I bid you do, get them dispatch'd,
    I will attend the Queen.

PISANIO: Madam, I shall.

                        Exeunt.

I.5 [I.4]

*Enter Philario, Iachimo, a Frenchman, a Dutchman,
and a Spaniard.*

IACHIMO: Believe it Sir, I have seen him in Britain; he
    was then of a crescent note, expected to prove so worthy,
    as since he hath been allowed the name of. But I could
    then have look'd on him, without the help of admiration,
    though the catalogue of his endowments had been
    tabled by his side, and I to peruse him by items.

PHILARIO: You speak of him when he was less furnish'd,
    than now he is, with that which makes him both with-
    out, and within.

FRENCHMAN: I have seen him in France: we had very

many there, could behold the Sun, with as firm eyes as he.

ACHIMO: This matter of marrying his King's Daughter, wherein he must be weighed rather by her value, than his own, words him (I doubt not) a great deal from the matter.

FRENCHMAN: And then his banishment.

ACHIMO: Ay, and the approbation of those that weep this lamentable divorce under her colours, are wonderfully to extend him, be it but to fortify her judgement, which else an easy battery might lay flat, for taking a beggar without less quality. But how comes it, he is to sojourn with you? How creeps acquaintance?

PHILARIO: His Father and I were soldiers together, to whom I have been often bound for no less than my life.

Enter Posthumus.

Here comes the Britain. Let him be so entertained amongst you, as suits with Gentlemen of your knowing, to a stranger of his quality. I beseech you all be better known to this Gentleman, whom I commend to you, as a noble Friend of mine. How worthy he is, I will leave to appear hereafter, rather than story him in his own hearing.

FRENCHMAN: Sir, we have known together in Orleans.

POSTHUMUS: Since when, I have been debtor to you for courtesies, which I will be ever to pay, and yet pay still.

FRENCHMAN: Sir, you o'er-rate my poor kindness, I was glad I did attone my Countryman and you: it had been pity you should have been put together, with so mortal a purpose, as then each bore, upon importance of so slight and trivial a nature.

POSTHUMUS: By your pardon Sir, I was then a young traveller, rather shunn'd to go even with what I heard, than in my every action to be guided by other's experiences: but upon my mended judgement (if I offend to say it is mended) my quarrel was not altogether slight.

FRENCHMAN: Faith yes, to be put to the arbitrement o
swords, and by such two, that would by all likelihoo
have confounded one the other, or have fall'n both.

IACHIMO: Can we with manners, ask what was th
difference?

FRENCHMAN: Safely, I think, 'twas a contention in public
which may (without contradiction) suffer the report
It was much like an argument that fell out last night
where each of us fell in praise of our Country-Mistresses
This Gentleman, at that time vouching (and upor
warrant of bloody affirmation) his to be more Fair
Virtuous, Wise, Chaste, Constant, Qualified, and les
attemptible than any, the rarest of our Ladies in France

IACHIMO: That Lady is not now living; or this Gentleman's opinion by this, worn out.

POSTHUMUS: She holds her virtue still, and I my mind.

IACHIMO: You must not so far prefer her, 'fore ours o
Italy.

POSTHUMUS: Being so far provok'd as I was in France:]
would abate her nothing, though I profess myself her
adorer, not her friend.

IACHIMO: As fair, and as good: a kind of hand in hand
comparison, had been something too fair, and too good
for any Lady in Britany; if she went before others.]
have seen as that diamond of yours out-lustres many]
have beheld, I could not believe she excelled many: but
I have not seen the most precious diamond that is, nor
you the Lady.

POSTHUMUS: I prais'd her, as I rated her: so do I my
stone.

IACHIMO: What do you esteem it at?

POSTHUMUS: More than the world enjoys.

IACHIMO: Either your unparagon'd Mistress is dead, or
she's out-priz'd by a trifle.

POSTHUMUS: You are mistaken: the one may be sold or

given, or if there were wealth enough for the purchases, or merit for the gift. The other is not a thing for sale, and only the gift of the Gods.

IACHIMO: Which the Gods have given you?

POSTHUMUS: Which by their graces I will keep.

IACHIMO: You may wear her in title yours: but you know strange fowl light upon neighbouring ponds. Your ring may be stol'n too, so your brace of un-prizable estimations, the one is but frail, and the other casual. A cunning thief, or a (that way) accomplish'd Courtier, would hazard the winning both of first and last.

POSTHUMUS: Your Italy, contains none so accomplish'd a Courtier to convince the honour of my Mistress: if in the holding or loss of that, you term her frail, I do nothing doubt you have store of thieves, notwithstand-ing I fear not my ring.

PHILARIO: Let us leave here, Gentlemen?

POSTHUMUS: Sir, with all my heart. This worthy Signior I thank him, makes no stranger of me, we are familiar at first.

IACHIMO: With five times so much conversation, I should get ground of your fair Mistress; make her go back, even to the yielding, had I admittance, and opportunity to friend.

POSTHUMUS: No, no.

IACHIMO: I dare thereupon pawn the moiety of my estate, to your ring, which in my opinion o'er-values it something: but I make my wager rather against your confidence, than her reputation. And to bar your offence herein too, I durst attempt it against any Lady in the world.

POSTHUMUS: You are a great deal abus'd in too bold a persuasion, and I doubt not you sustain what y'are worthy of, by your attempt.

IACHIMO: What's that?

POSTHUMUS: A repulse though your attempt (as you call it) deserve more; a punishment too.

PHILARIO: Gentlemen enough of this, it came in too suddenly, let it die as it was born, and I pray you be better acquainted.

IACHIMO: Would I had put my estate, and my neighbour's on th'approbation of what I have spoke,

POSTHUMUS: What Lady would you choose to assail?

IACHIMO: Yours, whom in constancy you think stands so safe. I will lay you ten thousand ducats to your ring, that commend me to the Court where your Lady is, with no more advantage than the opportunity of a second conference, and I will bring from thence, that honour of hers, which you imagine so reserv'd.

POSTHUMUS: I will wage against your gold, gold to it: My ring I hold dear as my finger, 'tis part of it.

IACHIMO: You are a friend, and therein the wiser: if you buy Ladies' flesh at a million a dram, you cannot preserve it from tainting; but I see you have some religion in you, that you fear.

POSTHUMUS: This is but a custom in your tongue: you bear a graver purpose I hope.

IACHIMO: I am the master of my speeches, and would undergo what's spoken, I swear.

POSTHUMUS: Will you? I shall but lend my diamond till your return: let there be covenants drawn between's. My Mistress exceeds in goodness, the hugeness of your unworthy thinking. I dare you to this match: here's my ring.

PHILARIO: I will have it no lay.

IACHIMO: By the Gods it is one: if I bring you no sufficient testimony that I have enjoy'd the dearest bodily part of your Mistress: my ten thousand ducats are yours, so is your diamond too: if I come off, and leave her in

such honour as you have trust in; She your jewel, this
your jewel, and my gold are yours: provided, I have
your commendation, for my more free entertainment.

POSTHUMUS: I embrace these conditions, let us have
articles betwixt us: only thus far you shall answer, if you
make your voyage upon her, and give me directly to understand, you have prevail'd, I am no further your
enemy, she is not worth our debate. If she remain un-
seduc'd, you not making it appear otherwise: for your ill
opinion, and th'assault you have made to her chastity,
you shall answer me with your sword.

IACHIMO: Your hand, a covenant: we will have these
things set down by lawful counsel, and straight away for
Britain, lest the bargain should catch cold, and starve: I
will fetch my gold, and have our two wagers recorded.

POSTHUMUS: Agreed.

FRENCHMAN: Will this hold, think you.

PHILARIO: Signor Iachimo will not from it.
Pray let us follow 'em.

Exeunt.

I.6 [I.5]

Enter Queen, Ladies, and Cornelius.

QUEEN: Whiles yet the dew's on ground,
Gather those flowers,
Make haste. Who has the note of them?

LADY: I Madam.

QUEEN: Dispatch.

Exit Ladies.

Now Master Doctor, have you brought those drugs?

CORNELIUS: Pleaseth your Highness, ay: here they are,
Madam:
But I beseech your Grace, without offence
(My conscience bids me ask) wherefore you have

Commanded of me these most poisonous compounds,
Which are the movers of a languishing death:
But though slow, deadly.

QUEEN: I wonder, Doctor,
Thou ask'st me such a question: Have I not been
Thy pupil long? Hast thou not learn'd me how
To make perfumes? Distill? Preserve? Yea so,
That our great King himself doth woo me oft
For my confections? Having thus far proceeded,
(Unless thou think'st me devilish) is't not meet
That I did amplify my judgement in
Other conclusions? I will try the forces
Of these thy compounds, on such creatures as
We count not worth the hanging (but none human)
To try the vigour of them, and apply
Allayments to their act, and by them gather
Their several virtues, and effects.

CORNELIUS: Your Highness
Shall from this practice, but make hard your heart:
Besides, the seeing these effects will be
Both noisome, and infectious.

QUEEN: O content thee.

Enter Pisanio.

Here comes a flattering rascal, upon him
Will I first work: He's for his Master,
And enemy to my Son. How now Pisanio?
Doctor, your service for this time is ended,
Take your own way.

CORNELIUS: I do suspect you, Madam,
But you shall do no harm.

QUEEN: Hark thee, a word.

CORNELIUS: I do not like her. She doth think she has
Strange ling'ring poisons: I do know her spirit,
And will not trust one of her malice, with
A drug of such damn'd nature. Those she has,

Will stupify and dull the sense awhile,
Which first (perchance) she'll prove on cats and dogs,
Then afterward up higher: but there is
No danger in what show of death it makes,
More than the locking up the spirits a time,
To be more fresh, reviving. She is fool'd,
With a most false effect: and I, the truer,
So to be false with her.

QUEEN: No further service, Doctor,
Until I send for thee.

CORNELIUS: I humbly take my leave.
                    Exit Cornelius.

QUEEN: Weeps she still (sayst thou?)
Dost thou think in time
She will not quench, and let instructions enter
Where folly now possesses? Do thou work:
When thou shalt bring me word she loves my Son,
I'll tell thee on the instant, thou art then
As great as is thy Master: Greater, for
His fortunes all lie speechless, and his name
Is at last gasp. Return he cannot, nor
Continue where he is: To shift his being,
Is to exchange one misery with another,
And every day that comes, comes to decay
A day's work in him. What shalt thou expect
To be depender on a thing that leans?
Who cannot be new built, nor has no friends
So much, as but to prop him? Thou tak'st up
Thou know'st not what: But take it for thy labour,
It is a thing I made, which hath the King
Five times redeem'd from death. I do not know
What is more cordial. Nay, I prithee take it.
It is an earnest of a farther good
That I mean to thee. Tell thy Mistress how
The case stands with her: do't, as from thyself;

Think what a chance thou changest on, but think
Thou hast thy Mistress still, to boot, my Son,
Who shall take notice of thee. I'll move the King
To any shape of thy preferment, such
As thou'lt desire: and then myself, I chiefly,
That set thee on to this desert, am bound
To load thy merit richly. Call my women.

Exit Pisanio.

Think on my words. A sly, and constant knave,
Not to be shak'd: the agent for his Master,
And the remembrancer of her, to hold
The hand-fast to her Lord. I have given him that,
Which if he take, shall quite unpeople her
Of Leigers for her sweet: and which, she after
Except she bend her humour, shall be assur'd
To taste of too.

Enter Pisanio, and Ladies.

So, so: Well done, well done:
The violets, cowslips, and the primroses
Bear to my closet: Fare thee well, Pisanio.
Think on my words.

Exit Queen, and Ladies.

PISANIO: And shall do:
But when to my good Lord, I prove untrue,
I'll choke myself: there's all I'll do for you.

Exit.

I.7 [I.6]

Enter Imogen alone.

IMOGEN: A Father cruel, and a Stepdame false,
A foolish Suitor to a wedded Lady,
That hath her Husband banish'd: O, that Husband,
My supreme crown of grief, and those repeated
Vexations of it. Had I been thief-stol'n,

As my two Brothers, happy: but most miserable
Is the desires that's glorious. Blessed be those
How mean so ere, that have their honest wills,
Which seasons comfort. Who may this be? Fie.

Enter Pisanio, and Iachimo.

PISANIO: Madam, a noble Gentleman of Rome, —
Comes from my Lord with letters.

IACHIMO: Change you, Madam:—
The worthy Leonatus is in safety,
And greets your Highness dearly.

IMOGEN: Thanks good Sir,
You're kindly welcome.

IACHIMO: All of her, that is out of door, most rich:
If she be furnish'd with a mind so rare
She is alone th'Arabian-Bird; and I
Have lost the wager. Boldness be my friend:
Arm me Audacity from head to foot,
Or like the Parthian I shall flying fight,
Rather directly fly.

Imogen reads.

*He is one of the noblest note, to whose kindnesses I am most
infinitely tied. Reflect upon him accordingly, as you value
your trust.*

Leonatus.

So far I read aloud.
But even the very middle of my heart
Is warm'd by th'rest, and take it thankfully.
You are as welcome (worthy Sir) as I
Have words to bid you, and shall find it so
In all that I can do.

IACHIMO: Thanks fairest Lady:
What are men mad? Hath Nature given them eyes
To see this vaulted arch, and the rich crop
Of sea and land, which can distinguish 'twixt

The fiery orbs above, and the twinn'd stones
Upon the number'd beach, and can we not
Partition make with spectacles so precious
Twixt fair, and foul?

IMOGEN: What makes your admiration?

IACHIMO: It cannot be i'th'eye: for apes, and monkeys
Twixt two such She's, would chatter this way, and
Contemn with mows the other. Nor i'th'judgement:
For idiots in this case of favour, would
Be wisely definite: Nor i'th'appetite.
Sluttery to such neat excellence, oppos'd
Should make desire vomit emptiness,
Not so allur'd to feed.

IMOGEN: What is the matter trow?

IACHIMO: The cloyed will:
That satiate yet unsatisfi'd desire, that tub
Both fill'd and running: Ravening first the lamb,
Longs after for the garbage.

IMOGEN: What, dear Sir,
Thus raps you? Are you well?

IACHIMO: Thanks Madam well: Beseech you Sir,
Desire my Man's abode, where I did leave him:
He's strange and peevish.

PISANIO: I was going Sir,
To give him welcome.

Exit.

IMOGEN: Continues well my Lord?
His health beseech you?

IACHIMO: Well, Madam.

IMOGEN: Is he dispos'd to mirth? I hope he is.

IACHIMO: Exceeding pleasant: none a stranger there,
So merry, and so gamesome: he is call'd
The Britain Reveller.

IMOGEN: When he was here
He did incline to sadness, and oft times

Not knowing why.

IACHIMO: I never saw him sad.
There is a Frenchman his companion, one
An eminent Monsieur, that it seems much loves
A Gallian Girl at home. He furnaces
The thick sighs from him; whiles the jolly Britain,
(Your Lord I mean) laughs from's free lungs: cries oh,
Can my sides hold, to think that man who knows
By history, report, or his own proof
What woman is, yea what she cannot choose
But must be: will's free hours languish:
For assured bondage?

IMOGEN: Will my Lord say so?

IACHIMO: Ay Madam, with his eyes in flood with
laughter,
It is a recreation to be by
And hear him mock the Frenchman:
But Heavens know some men are much to blame.

IMOGEN: Not he I hope.

IACHIMO: Not he:
But yet Heaven's bounty towards him, might
Be us'd more thankfully. In himself 'tis much;
In you, which I account his beyond all talents.
Whil'st I am bound to wonder, I am bound
To pity too.

IMOGEN: What do you pity Sir?

IACHIMO: Two creatures heartily.

IMOGEN: Am I one Sir?
You look on me: what wrack discern you in me
Deserves your pity?

IACHIMO: Lamentable: what
To hide me from the radiant Sun, and solace
I'th'dungeon by a snuff.

IMOGEN: I pray you Sir,
Deliver with more openness your answers

To my demands. Why do you pity me?

IACHIMO: That others do,
(I was about to say) enjoy your – but
It is an office of the Gods to venge it,
Not mine to speak on't.

IMOGEN: You do seem to know
Something of me, or what concerns me; pray you
Since doubting things go ill, often hurts more
Than to be sure they do. For certainties
Either are past remedies; or timely knowing,
The remedy then born. Discover to me
What both you spur and stop.

IACHIMO: Had I this cheek
To bathe my lips upon: this hand, whose touch,
(Whose every touch) would force the feeler's soul
To'th'oath of loyalty. This object, which
Takes prisoner the wild motion of mine eye,
Fixing it only here, should I (damn'd then)
Slaver with lips as common as the stairs
That mount the Capitol: Join grips, with hands
Made hard with hourly falsehood (falsehood as
With labour:) then by peeping in an eye
Base and illustrious as the smoky light
That's fed with stinking tallow: it were fit
That all the plagues of Hell should at one time
Encounter such revolt.

IMOGEN: My Lord, I fear
Has forgot Britain.

IACHIMO: And himself, not I
Inclin'd to this intelligence, pronounce
The beggary of his change: but 'tis your graces
That from my mutest conscience, to my tongue,
Charms this report out.

IMOGEN: Let me hear no more.

IACHIMO: O dearest Soul: your cause doth strike my heart

With pity, that doth make me sick. A Lady
So fair, and fasten'd to an Empery
Would make the great'st King double, to be partner'd
With tomboys hir'd, with that self exhibition
Which your own coffers yield: with diseas'd ventures
That play with all infirmities for gold,
Which rottenness can lend Nature. Such boil'd stuff
As well might poison poison. Be reveng'd,
Or she that bore you, was no Queen, and you
Recoil from your great Stock.

IMOGEN: Reveng'd: *Innoc. strike attit.*
How should I be reveng'd? If this be true,
(As I have such a heart, that both mine ears
Must not in haste abuse) if it be true,
How should I be reveng'd?

IACHIMO: Should he make me *Proper*
Live like Diana's Priest, betwixt cold sheets,
Whiles he is vaulting variable ramps
In your despite, upon your purse: revenge it.
I dedicate myself to your sweet pleasure,
More noble than that runnagate to your bed,
And will continue fast to your affection,
Still close, as sure.

IMOGEN: What hoa, Pisanio?

IACHIMO: Let me my service tender on your lips. *Menacing*

IMOGEN: Away, I do condemn mine ears, that have *Fright*
So long attended thee. If thou wert honourable
Thou would'st have told this tale for virtue, not *clutch cloak*
For such an end thou seek'st, as base, as strange:
Thou wrong'st a Gentleman, who is as far
From thy report, as thou from honour: and
Solicits here a Lady, that disdains
Thee, and the Devil alike. What hoa, Pisanio?
The King my Father shall be made acquainted
Of thy assault: if he shall think it fit,

A saucy Stranger in his Court, to mart
As in a Romish Stew, and to expound
His beastly mind to us; he hath a Court
He little cares for, and a Daughter, who
He not respects at all. What hoa, Pisanio?

IACHIMO: O happy Leonatus I may say,
The credit that thy Lady hath of thee
Deserves thy trust, and thy most perfect goodness
Her assur'd credit. Blessed live you long,
A Lady to the worthiest Sir, that ever
Country call'd his; and you his Mistress, only
For the most worthiest fit. Give me your pardon,
I have spoke this to know if your affiance
Were deeply rooted, and shall make your Lord,
That which he is, new o'er: And he is one
The truest manner'd: such a holy witch,
That he enchants societies into him:
Half all men's hearts are his.

IMOGEN: You make amends.

IACHIMO: He sits mongst men, like a defended God;
He hath a kind of honour sets him off,
More than a mortal seeming. Be not angry
(Most mighty Princess) that I have adventur'd
To try your taking of a false report, which hath
Honour'd with confirmation your great judgement,
In the election of a Sir, so rare,
Which you know, cannot err. The love I bear him,
Made me to fan you thus, but the Gods made you
(Unlike all others) chaffless. Pray your pardon.

IMOGEN: All's well Sir:
Take my power i'th'Court for yours.

IACHIMO: My humble thanks: I had almost forgot
T'entreat your Grace, but in a small request,
And yet of moment too, for it concerns:
Your Lord, myself, and other noble friends

Are partners in the business.

IMOGEN: Pray what is't?

IACHIMO: Some dozen Romans of us, and your Lord
(The best feather of our wing) have mingled sums
To buy a present for the Emperor:
Which I (the factor for the rest) have done
In France: 'tis plate of rare device, and jewels
Of rich, and exquisite form, their values great,
And I am something curious, being strange
To have them in safe stowage: May it please you
To take them in protection.

IMOGEN: Willingly:
And pawn mine honour for their safety, since
My Lord hath interest in them, I will keep them
In my bed-chamber.

IACHIMO: They are in a trunk
Attended by my men: I will make bold
To send them to you, only for this night:
I must abroad tomorrow.

IMOGEN: O no, no.

IACHIMO: Yes I beseech: or I shall short my word
By length'ning my return. From Gallia,
I cross'd the seas on purpose, and on promise
To see your Grace.

IMOGEN: I thank you for your pains:
But not away tomorrow.

IACHIMO: O I must Madam.
Therefore I shall beseech you, if you please
To greet your Lord with writing, do't tonight,
I have outstood my time, which is material
To'th'tender of our present.

IMOGEN: I will write:
Send your trunk to me, it shall safe be kept,
And truly yielded you: you're very welcome.
                    Exeunt.

II. 1

Enter Cloten, and the two Lords.

CLOTEN: Was there ever man had such luck? when I kiss'd the jack upon an up-cast, to be hit away? I had a hundred pound on't: and then a whorson Jack-an-Apes, must take me up for swearing, as if I borrowed mine oaths of him, and might not spend them at my pleasure.

1 LORD: What got he by that? you have broke his pate with your bowl.

2 LORD: If his wit had been like him that broke it: it would have run all out.

CLOTEN: When a Gentleman is dispos'd to swear: it is not for any standers by to curtall his oaths. Ha?

2 LORD: No my Lord; nor crop the ears of them.

CLOTEN: Whorson dog: I gave him satisfaction? would he had been one of my Rank.

2 LORD: To have smell'd like a fool.

CLOTEN: I am not vex'd more at any thing in th'earth: a pox on't. I had rather not be so Noble as I am: they dare not fight with me, because of the Queen my Mother: every Jack-Slave hath his belly full of fighting, and I must go up and down like a cock, that no body can match.

2 LORD: You are cock and capon too, and you crow cock, with your comb on.

CLOTEN: Sayest thou?

2 LORD: It is not fit your Lordship should undertake every companion, that you give offence too.

CLOTEN: No, I know that: but it is fit I should commit offence to my inferiors.

2 LORD: Ay, it is fit for your Lordship only.

CLOTEN: Why so I say.

1 LORD: Did you hear of a Stranger that's come to Court night?

CLOTEN: A Stranger, and I not know on't?

2 LORD: He's a strange fellow himself, and knows it not.

LORD: There's an Italian come, and 'tis thought one of
Leonatus' friends.

CLOTEN: Leonatus? A banished Rascal; and he's another,
whatsoever he be. Who told you of this Stranger?

1 LORD: One of your Lordship's Pages.

CLOTEN: Is it fit I went to look upon him? Is there no
derogation in't?

2 LORD: You cannót derogate my Lord.

CLOTEN: Not easily I think.

2 LORD: You are a fool granted, therefore your issues
being foolish do not derogate.

CLOTEN: Come, I'll go see this Italian: what I have lost
today at bowls, I'll win tonight of him. Come: go.

2 LORD: I'll attend your Lordship.

Exit.

That such a crafty Devil as is his Mother
Should yield the world this Ass: A woman, that
Bears all down with her brain, and this her Son,
Cannot take two from twenty for his heart,
And leave eighteen. Alas poor Princess,
Thou divine Imogen, what thou endur'st,
Betwixt a Father by thy Step-dame govern'd,
A Mother hourly coining plots: A Wooer,
More hateful than the foul expulsion is
Of thy dear Husband. Then that horrid act
Of the divorce, he'd make the Heavens hold firm
The walls of thy dear honour. Keep unshak'd
That temple thy fair mind, that thou mayst stand
T'enjoy thy banish'd Lord; and this great Land.

Exeunt.

II.2

Enter Imogen, in her Bed, and a Lady.

IMOGEN: Who's there: My woman: Helene?

LADY: Please you Madam.

IMOGEN: What hour is it?

LADY: Almost midnight, Madam.

IMOGEN: I have read three hours then:
  Mine eyes are weak,
  Fold down the leaf where I have left: to bed.
  Take not away the taper, leave it burning:
  And if thou canst awake by four o'th'clock,
  I prithee call me: Sleep hath seiz'd me wholly.
  To your protection I commend me, Gods,
  From Faeries, and the Tempters of the night,
  Guard me beseech ye.

Sleeps.

Iachimo from the Trunk.

IACHIMO: The crickets sing, and man's o'er-labour'd
  sense
  Repairs itself by rest: Our Tarquin thus
  Did softly press the rushes, ere he waken'd
  The chastity he wounded. Cytherea,
  How bravely thou becom'st thy bed; fresh Lily,
  And whiter than the sheets: that I might touch,
  But kiss, one kiss. Rubies unparagon'd,
  How dearly they do't: 'Tis her breathing that
  Perfumes the chamber thus: the flame o'th'taper
  Bows toward her, and would under-peep her lids.
  To see th'enclosed lights, now canopied
  Under these windows, white and azure lac'd
  With blue of Heaven's own tinct. But my design.
  To note the chamber, I will write all down,
  Such, and such pictures: There the window, such

Th'adornment of her bed; the arras, figures,
Why such, and such: and the contents o'th'story.
Ah, but some natural notes about her body,
Above ten thousand meaner moveables
Would testify, t'enrich mine inventory.
O sleep, thou Ape of death, lie dull upon her,
And be her sense but as a monument,
Thus in a Chapel lying. Come off, come off;
As slippery as the Gordian-knot was hard.
'Tis mine, and this will witness outwardly,
As strongly as the conscience does within:
To'th'madding of her Lord. On her left breast
A mole cinque-spotted: Like the crimson drops
I'th'bottom of a cowslip. Here's a voucher,
Stronger than ever Law could make; this secret
Will force him think I have pick'd the lock, and ta'en
The treasure of her honour. No more: to what end?
Why should I write this down, that's riveted,
Screw'd to my memory. She hath been reading late,
The Tale of Tereus, here the leaf's turn'd down
Where Philomele gave up. I have enough,
To'th'trunk again, and shut the spring of it.
Swift, swift, you Dragons of the night, that dawning
May bare the Raven's eye: I lodge in fear,
Though this a heavenly Angel: hell is here.
                    Clock strikes.
One, two, three: time, time.
                    Exit.

II. 3

Enter Cloten, and Lords.

I LORD: Your Lordship is the most patient man in loss,
the most coldest that ever turn'd up ace.

CLOTEN: It would make any man cold to lose.

1 LORD: But not every man patient after the noble temper of your Lordship: You are most hot, and furious when you win.

CLOTEN: Winning will put any man into courage: if I could get this foolish Imogen, I should have gold enough: it's almost morning, is't not?

1 LORD: Day, my Lord.

CLOTEN: I would this Music would come: I am advised to give her music a-mornings, they say it will penetrate.

Enter Musicians.

Come on, tune: If you can penetrate her with your fingering, so: we'll try with tongue too: if none will do, let her remain: but I'll never give o'er. First, a very excellent good conceited thing; after a wonderful sweet air, with admirable rich words to it, and then let her consider.

SONG

Hark, hark, the Lark at Heaven's gate sings,
*   and Phoebus gins arise,*
His steeds to water at those springs
*   on chalic'd flowers that lies:*
And winking Mary-buds begin to ope their golden eyes
With every thing that pretty is, my Lady sweet arise:
*   Arise, arise.*

So, get you gone: if this penetrate, I will consider your music the better; if it do not, it is a voice in her ears which horse-hairs, and calves'-guts, nor the voice of unpaved eunuch to boot, can never amend.

Enter Cymbeline, and Queen.

2 LORD: Here comes the King.

CLOTEN: I am glad I was up so late, for that's the reason I was up so early: he cannot choose but take this service I have done, fatherly. Good morrow to your Majesty, and to my gracious Mother.

CYMBELINE: Attend you here the door of our stern daughter

Will she not forth?

CLOTEN: I have assail'd her with musics, but she vouch-
safes no notice.

CYMBELINE: The exile of her Minion is too new,
She hath not yet forgot him, some more time
Must wear the print of his remembrance on't.
And then she's yours.

QUEEN: You are most bound to'th'King,
Who lets go by no vantages, that may
Prefer you to his daughter: Frame yourself
To orderly solicity, and be friended
With aptness of the season: make denials
Increase your services: so seem, as if
You were inspir'd to do those duties which
You tender to her: that you in all obey her,
Save when command to your dismission tends,
And therein you are senseless.

CLOTEN: Senseless? Not so.

MESSENGER: So like you (Sir) Ambassadors from Rome;
The one is Caius Lucius.

CYMBELINE: A worthy Fellow,
Albeit he comes on angry purpose now;
But that's no fault of his: we must receive him
According to the honour of his Sender,
And towards himself, his goodness fore-spent on us
We must extend our notice: Our dear Son,
When you have given good morning to your Mistress,
Attend the Queen, and us, we shall have need
T'employ you towards this Roman.
Come our Queen.

Exeunt.

CLOTEN: If she be up, I'll speak with her: if not
Let her lie still, and dream: by your leave hoa,
I know her women are about her: what
If I do line one of their hands, 'tis gold

Which buys admittance (oft it doth) yea, and makes
Diana's Rangers false themselves, yield up
Their deer to'th'stand o'th'stealer: and 'tis gold
Which makes the true-man kill'd, and saves the thief:
Nay, sometime hangs both thief, and true-man: what
Can it not do, and undo? I will make
One of her women lawyer to me, for
I yet not understand the case myself.
By your leave.

Knocks.
Enter a Lady.

LADY: Who's there that knocks?
CLOTEN: A Gentleman.
LADY: No more.
CLOTEN: Yes, and a Gentlewoman's Son.
LADY: That's more
    Than some whose tailors are as dear as yours.
    Can justly boast of: what's your Lordship's pleasure?
CLOTEN: Your Lady's person, is she ready?
LADY: Ay, to keep her chamber.
CLOTEN: There is gold for you,
    Sell me your good report.
LADY: How my good name? or to report of you
    What I shall think is good. The Princess.

Enter Imogen.

CLOTEN: Good morrow fairest, Sister your sweet hand.
IMOGEN: Good morrow Sir, you lay out too much pains
    For purchasing but trouble: the thanks I give,
    Is telling you that I am poor of thanks,
    And scarce can spare them.
CLOTEN: Still I swear I love you.
IMOGEN: If you but said so, 'twere as deep with me:
    If you swear still, your recompence is still
    That I regard it not.
CLOTEN: This is no answer.

IMOGEN: But that you shall not say, I yield being silent,
　I would not speak. I pray you spare me, 'faith
　I shall unfold equal discourtesy
　To your best kindness: one of your great knowing
　Should learn (being taught) forbearance.

CLOTEN: To leave you in your madness, 'twere my sin,
　I will not.

IMOGEN: Fools are not mad folks. ✗

CLOTEN: Do you call me fool?

IMOGEN: As I am mad I do:
　If you'll be patient, I'll no more be mad,
　That cures us both. I am much sorry (Sir)
　You put me to forget a Lady's manners
　By being so verbal: and learn now, for all,
　That I which know my heart, do here pronounce
　By th'very truth of it, I care not for you,
　And am so near the lack of charity
　To accuse myself, I hate you: which I had rather
　You felt, than make't my boast.

CLOTEN: You sin against
　Obedience, which you owe your Father, for
　The contract you pretend with that base wretch,
　One, bred of alms, and foster'd with cold dishes,
　With scraps o'th'Court: It is no contract, none;
　And though it be allowed in meaner parties
　(Yet who than he more mean) to knit their souls
　(On whom there is no more dependency
　But brats and beggary) in self-figur'd knot,
　Yet you are curb'd from that enlargement, by
　The consequence o'th'Crown, and must not soil
　The precious note of it; with a base Slave,
　A hilding for a livery, a squire's cloth,
　A pantler; not so eminent.

IMOGEN: Profane fellow:
　Wert thou the Son of Jupiter, and no more,

But what thou art besides: thou were't too base,
To be his groom: thou were't dignified enough
Even to the point of envy. If 'twere made
Comparative for your virtues, to be styl'd
The under-hangman of his Kingdom; and hated
For being preferr'd so well.

CLOTEN: The South-Fog rot him.

IMOGEN: He never can meet more mischance, than come
To be but nam'd of thee. His mean'st garment
That ever hath but clipp'd his body; is dearer
In my respect, than all the hairs above thee,
Were they all made such men: How now Pisanio?

Enter Pisanio.

CLOTEN: His garments? Now the devil.

IMOGEN: To Dorothy my woman hie thee presently.

CLOTEN: His garment?

IMOGEN: I am sprighted with a Fool,
Frighted, and anger'd worse: Go bid my woman
Search for a jewel, that too casually
Hath left mine arm: it was thy Master's. Shrew me
If I would lose it for a revenue,
Of any King's in Europe. I do think,
I saw't this morning: Confident I am.
Last night 'twas on mine arm; I kiss'd it,
I hope it be not gone, to tell my Lord
That I kiss aught but he.

PISANIO: 'Twill not be lost.

IMOGEN: I hope so: go and search.

CLOTEN: You have abus'd me:
His meanest garment?

IMOGEN: Ay, I said so Sir,
If you will make't an action, call witness to't.

CLOTEN: I will inform your Father.

IMOGEN: Your Mother too:
She's my good Lady; and will conceive, I hope

But the worst of me. So I leave your Sir,
To'th'worst of discontent.

Exit.

CLOTEN: I'll be reveng'd:
His mean'st garment? Well.

Exit.

II.4

Enter Posthumus, and Philario.

POSTHUMUS: Fear it not Sir: I would I were so sure
  To win the King, as I am bold, her honour
  Will remain hers.

PHILARIO: What means do you make to him?

POSTHUMUS: Not any: but abide the change of Time,
  Quake in the present winter's state, and wish
  That warmer days would come: In these fear'd hope
  I barely gratify your love; they failing
  I must die much your debtor.

PHILARIO: Your very goodness, and your company,
  O'er-pays all I can do. By this your King,
  Hath heard of Great Augustus: Caius Lucius,
  Will do's commission throughly. And I think
  He'll grant the Tribute: send th'arrearages,
  Or look upon our Romans, whose remembrance
  Is yet fresh in their grief.

POSTHUMUS: I do believe
  (Statist though I am none, nor like to be)
  That this will prove a War; and you shall hear
  The Legion now in Gallia, sooner landed
  In our not-fearing Britain, than have tidings
  Of any penny Tribute paid. Our Countrymen
  Are men more order'd, than when Julius Caesar
  Smil'd at their lack of skill, but found their courage
  Worthy his frowning at. Their discipline,

(Now wing-led with their courages) will make known
To their approvers, they are people, such
That mend upon the world.

Enter Iachimo.

PHILARIO: See Iachimo.

POSTHUMUS: The swiftest hearts, have posted you by
    land;
And winds of all the corners kiss'd your sails,
To make your vessel nimble.

PHILARIO: Welcome Sir.

POSTHUMUS: I hope the briefness of your answer, made
The speediness of your return.

IACHIMO: Your Lady,
Is one of the fairest that I have look'd upon –

POSTHUMUS: And therewithal the best, or let her beauty
Look thorough a casement to allure false hearts,
And be false with them.

IACHIMO: Here are letters for you.

POSTHUMUS: Their tenure good I trust.

IACHIMO: 'Tis very like.

POSTHUMUS: Was Caius Lucius in the Britain Court,
When you were there?

IACHIMO: He was expected then,
But not approach'd.

POSTHUMUS: All is well yet,
Sparkles this stone as it was wont, or is't not
Too dull for your good wearing?

IACHIMO: If I have lost it,
I should have lost the worth of it in gold,
I'll make a journey twice as far, t'enjoy
A second night of such sweet shortness, which
Was mine in Britain, for the ring is won.

POSTHUMUS: The stone's too hard to come by.

IACHIMO: Not a whit,
Your Lady being so easy.

POSTHUMUS: Make note Sir
  Your loss, your sport: I hope you know that we
  Must not continue friends.
IACHIMO: Good Sir, we must
  If you keep covenant: had I not brought
  The knowledge of your Mistress home, I grant
  We were to question farther; but I now
  Profess myself the winner of her honour,
  Together with your ring; and not the wronger
  Of her, or you having proceeded but
  By both your wills.
POSTHUMUS: If you can mak't apparent
  That you have tasted her in bed; my hand,
  And ring is yours. If not, the foul opinion
  You had of her pure honours gains, or loses,
  Your sword, or mine, or masterless leave both
  To who shall find them.
IACHIMO: Sir, my circumstances
  Being so near the truth, as I will make them,
  Must first induce you to believe; whose strength
  I will confirm with oath, which I doubt not
  You'll give me leave to spare, when you shall find
  You need it not.
POSTHUMUS: Proceed.
IACHIMO: First, her bed-chamber
  (Where I confess I slept not, but profess
  Had that was well worth watching) it was hang'd
  With tapestry of silk, and silver, the story
  Proud Cleopatra, when she met her Roman,
  And Cydnus swell'd above the banks, or for
  The press of boats, or price. A piece of work
  So bravely done, so rich, that it did strive
  In workmanship, and value, which I wonder'd
  Could be so rarely, and exactly wrought
  Since the true life on't was—

POSTHUMUS: This is true:
    And this you might have heard of here, by me,
    Or by some other.
IACHIMO: More particulars
    Must justify my knowledge.
POSTHUMUS: So they must,
    Or do your honour injury.
IACHIMO: The chimney
    Is south the chamber, and the chimney-piece
    Chaste Dian, bathing: never saw I figures
    So likely to report themselves; the cutter
    Was as another Nature dumb, out-went her,
    Motion, and breath left out.
POSTHUMUS: This is a thing
    Which you might from relation likewise reap,
    Being, as it is, much spoke of.
IACHIMO: The roof o'th'chamber,
    With golden cherubins is fretted. Her andirons
    (I had forgot them) were two winking Cupids
    Of silver, each on one foot standing, nicely
    Depending on their brands.
POSTHUMUS: This is her honour:
    Let it be granted you have seen all this (and praise
    Be given to your remembrance) the description
    Of what is in her chamber, nothing saves
    The wager you have laid.
IACHIMO: Then if you can
    Be pale, I beg but leave to air this jewel: See,
    And now 'tis up again: it must be married
    To that your diamond, I'll keep them.
POSTHUMUS: Jove —
    Once more let me behold it: Is it that
    Which I left with her?
IACHIMO: Sir (I thank her) that
    She stripp'd it from her arm: I see her yet:

Her pretty action, did out-sell her gift,
And yet enrich'd it too: she gave it me,
And said, she priz'd it once.

POSTHUMUS: May be, she pluck'd it off
To send it me.

IACHIMO: She writes so to you? doth she?

POSTHUMUS: O no, no, no, 'tis true. Here, take this
too,
It is a Basilisk unto mine eye,
Kills me to look on't: Let there be no Honour,
Where there is Beauty: Truth, where semblance: Love,
Where there's another man. The vows of Women,
Of no more bondage be, to where they are made,
Than they are to their virtues, which is nothing:
O, above measure false.

PHILARIO: Have patience Sir,
And take your ring again, 'tis not yet won:
It may be probable she lost it: or
Who knows if one her women, being corrupted
Hath stolen it from her.

POSTHUMUS: Very true,
And so I hope he came by't: back my ring,
Render to me some corporal sign about her
More evident than this: for this was stolen.

IACHIMO: By Jupiter, I had it from her arm.

POSTHUMUS: Hark you, he swears: by Jupiter he swears.
'Tis true, nay keep the ring; 'tis true: I am sure
She would not lose it: her attendants are
All sworn, and honourable: they induc'd to steal it?
And by a Stranger? No, he hath enjoy'd her,
The cognizance of her incontinency
Is this: she hath bought the name of Whore, thus dearly
There, take thy hire, and all the Fiends of Hell
Divide themselves between you.

PHILARIO: Sir, be patient:

This is not strong enough to be believ'd
Of one persuaded well of.

POSTHUMUS: Never talk on't:
She hath been colted by him.

IACHIMO: If you seek
For further satisfying, under her breast
(Worthy her pressing) lies a mole, right proud
Of that most delicate lodging. By my life
I kiss'd it, and it gave me present hunger
To feed again, though full. You do remember
This stain upon her?

POSTHUMUS: Ay, and it doth confirm
Another stain, as big as Hell can hold,
Were there no more but it.

IACHIMO: Will you hear more?

POSTHUMUS: Spare your arithmetic,
Never count the turns: Once, and a million.

IACHIMO: I'll be sworn.

POSTHUMUS: No swearing:
If you will swear you have not done't, you lie,
And I will kill thee, if thou do'st deny
Thou'st made me Cuckold.

IACHIMO: I'll deny nothing.

POSTHUMUS: O that I had her here, to tear her limb-meal:
I will go there and do't, i'th'Court, before
Her Father. I'll do something.

Exit.

PHILARIO: Quite besides
The government of Patience. You have won:
Let's follow him, and pervert the present wrath
He hath against himself.

IACHIMO: With all my heart.

Exeunt.

[II. 5]

Enter Posthumus.

POSTHUMUS: Is there no way for Men to be, but Women
Must be half-workers? We are all Bastards, *when*
And that most venerable man, which I
Did call my Father, was, I know not where
When I was stamp'd. Some coiner with his tools
Made me a counterfeit: yet my Mother seem'd
The Dian of that time: so doth my Wife
The non-pareill of this. Oh Vengeance, Vengeance! X
Me of my lawful pleasure she restrain'd,
And pray'd me oft forbearance: did it with
A pudency so rosy, the sweet view on't
Might well have warm'd old Saturn;
That I thought her
As chaste, as un-sunn'd snow. Oh, all the Devils!
This yellow Iachimo in an hour, was't not?
Or less; at first? Perchance he spoke not, but
Like a full acorn'd boar, a Jarmen one,
Cri'd oh, and mounted; found no opposition
But what he look'd for, should oppose, and she
Should from encounter guard. Could I find out
The Woman's part in me, for there's no motion
That tends to vice in man, but I affirm
It is the Woman's part: be it lying, note it, X
The woman's: Flattering, hers; Deceiving, hers:
Lust, and rank thoughts, hers, hers: Revenges hers:
Ambitions, Covetings, change of Prides, Disdain,
Nice-longing, Slanders, Mutability;
All faults that name, nay, that Hell knows,
Why hers, in part, or all: but rather all: For even to
Vice
They are not constant, but are changing still;

c

One vice, but of a minute old, for one
Not half so old as that. I'll write against them,
Detest them, curse them: yet 'tis greater skill
In a true hate, to pray they have their will:
The very Devils cannot plague them better.

Exit.

III. 1

Enter in State, Cymbeline, Queen, Cloten,
and Lords at one door, and at another, Caius Lucius,
and Attendants.

CYMBELINE: Now say, what would Augustus Caesar
 with us?

LUCIUS: When Julius Caesar (whose remembrance yet
 Lives in men's eyes, and will to ears and tongues
 Be theme, and hearing ever) was in this Britain,
 And conquer'd it, Cassibulan thine Uncle
 (Famous in Caesar's praises, no whit less
 Than in his feats deserving it) for him,
 And his succession, granted Rome a Tribute,
 Yearly three thousand pounds; which (by thee) lately
 Is left untender'd.

QUEEN: And to kill the marvel,
 Shall be so ever.

CLOTEN: There be many Caesars,
 Ere such another Julius: Britain's a world
 By itself, and we will nothing pay
 For wearing our own noses.

QUEEN: That opportunity
 Which then they had to take from's, to resume
 We have again. Remember Sir, my Liege,
 The Kings your Ancestors, together with
 The natural bravery of your Isle, which stands
 As Neptune's Park, ribb'd, and pal'd in

With oaks unscaleable, and roaring waters,
With sands that will not bear your Enemies' boats,
But suck them up to'th'top-mast. A kind of conquest
Caesar made here, but made not here his brag
Of Came, and Saw, and Over-came: with shame
(The first that ever touch'd him) he was carried
From off our coast, twice beaten: and his shipping
(Poor ignorant baubles) on our terrible seas
Like egg-shells mov'd upon their surges, crack'd
As easily 'gainst our rocks. For joy whereof,
The fam'd Cassibulan, who was once at point
(Oh giglet Fortune) to master Caesar's sword,
Made Lud's-Town with rejoicing fires bright,
And Britains strut with courage.

CLOTEN: Come, there's no more tribute to be paid: our
  Kingdom is stronger than it was at that time: and (as I
  said) there is no mo such Caesars, other of them may
  have crook'd noses, but to owe such straight arms, none.

CYMBELINE: Son, let your Mother end.

CLOTEN: We have yet many among us, can gripe as hard
  as Cassibulan, I do not say I am one: but I have a hand.
  Why Tribute? Why should we pay Tribute? If Caesar
  can hide the Sun from us with a blanket, or put the Moon
  in his pocket, we will pay him Tribute for light: else Sir,
  no more Tribute pray you now.

CYMBELINE: You must know,
  Till the injurious Romans, did extort
  This Tribute from us, we were free. Caesar's ambition,
  Which swell'd so much, that it did almost stretch
  The sides o'th'World, against all colour here,
  Did put the yoke upon's; which to shake off
  Becomes a warlike people, whom we reckon
  Ourselves to be, we do. Say then to Caesar,
  Our Ancestor was that Mulmutius, which
  Ordain'd our Laws, whose use the sword of Caesar

Hath too much mangled; whose repair, and franchise,
Shall (by the power we hold) be our good deed,
Though Rome be therefore angry. Mulmutius made ou
  laws
Who was the first of Britain, which did put
His brows within a golden crown, and call'd
Himself a King.

LUCIUS: I am sorry Cymbeline,
That I am to pronounce Augustus Caesar
(Caesar, that hath moe Kings his Servants, than
Thyself domestick Officers) thine Enemy:
Receive it from me then. War, and Confusion
In Caesar's name pronounce I 'gainst thee: Look
For fury, not to be resisted. Thus defied,
I thank thee for myself.

CYMBELINE: Thou art welcome Caius,
Thy Caesar knighted me; my youth I spent
Much under him; of him, I gather'd honour,
Which he, to seek of me again, perforce,
Behooves me keep at utterance. I am perfect,
That the Pannonians and Dalmatians, for
Their liberties are now in arms: a precedent
Which not to read, would show the Britains cold:
So Caesar shall not find them.

LUCIUS: Let proof speak.

CLOTEN: His Majesty bids you welcome. Make pastime
with us, a day, or two, or longer: if you seek us afterwards in other terms, you shall find us in our saltwater
Girdle: if you beat us out of it, it is yours: if you fall in
the adventure, our crows shall fare the better for you:
and there's an end.

LUCIUS: So sir.

CYMBELINE: I know your Master's pleasure, and he mine:
All the remain, is welcome.

               Exeunt.

III.2

Enter Pisanio reading of a Letter.

PISANIO: How? of Adultery? Wherefore write you not
  What Monsters her accuse? Leonatus:
  Oh Master, what a strange infection
  Is fallen into thy ear? What false Italian,
  (As poisonous tongu'd, as handed) hath prevail'd
  On thy too ready hearing? Disloyal? No.
  She's punish'd for her truth; and undergoes
  More goddess-like, than wife-like; such assaults
  As would take in some virtue. Oh my Master,
  Thy mind to her, is now as low, as were
  Thy fortunes. How? That I should murther her,
  Upon the love, and truth, and vows; which I
  Have made to thy command? I her? Her blood?
  If it be so, to do good service, never
  Let me be counted serviceable. How look I,
  That I should seem to lack humanity,
  So much as this fact comes to? Do't: The Letter.
  That I have sent her, by her own command,
  Shall give thee opportunity. Oh damn'd paper,
  Black as the ink that's on thee: senseless bauble,
  Art thou a foedary for this act; and look'st
  So virgin-like without? Lo here she comes.

Enter Imogen.

  I am ignorant in what I am commanded.

IMOGEN: How now Pisanio?

PISANIO: Madam, here is a letter from my Lord.

IMOGEN: Who, thy Lord? That is my Lord Leonatus?
  Oh, learn'd indeed were that Astronomer
  That knew the stars, as I his characters,
  He'ld lay the future open. You good Gods,
  Let what is here contain'd, relish of love,

Of my Lord's health, of his content: yet not
That we two are asunder, let that grieve him;
Some griefs are medcinable, that is one of them,
For it doth physick Love, of his content,
All but in that. Good wax, thy leave: bless'd be
You bees that make these locks of counsel. Lovers,
And men in dangerous bonds pray not alike,
Though forfeitors you cast in prison, yet
You clasp young Cupid's tables: good news Gods.

Justice, and your Father's wrath (should he take me in his
Dominion) could not be so cruel to me, as you: (oh the
dearest of Creatures) would even renew me with your eyes
Take notice that I am in Cambria at Milford-Haven: what
your own Love, will out of this advise you, follow. So he
wishes you all happiness, that remains loyal to his Vow, and
your increasing in Love.

                              Leonatus Posthumus.

Oh for a horse with wings: Hear'st thou Pisanio?
He is at Milford-Haven: Read, and tell me
How far 'tis thither. If one of mean affairs
May plod it in a week, why may not I
Glide thither in a day? Then true Pisanio,
Who long'st like me, to see thy Lord: who long'st
(Oh let me bate) but not like me: yet long'st
But in a fainter kind. Oh not like me:
For mine's beyond, beyond: say, and speak thick
(Love's Councillor should fill the bores of hearing,
To'th'smothering of the sense) how far it is
To this same blessed Milford. And by'th'way
Tell me how Wales was made so happy, as I
T'inherit such a haven. But first of all,
How we may steal from hence: and for the gap
That we shall make in time, from our hence-going,
And our return, to excuse: but first, how get hence.

Why should excuse be born or e'er begot?
We'll talk of that hereafter. Prithee speak,
How many store of miles may we well rid
Twixt hour, and hour?

PISANIO: One score 'twixt sun, and sun,
  Madam's enough for you: and too much too.

IMOGEN: Why, one that rode to's execution man,
  Could never go so slow: I have heard of riding wagers,
  Where horses have been nimbler than the sands
  That run i'th'clock's behalf. But this is foolery,
  Go, bid my Woman feign a sickness, say
  She'll home to her Father; and provide me presently
  A riding suit: No costlier than would fit
  A Franklin's housewife.

PISANIO: Madam, you're best consider.

IMOGEN: I see before me (Man) nor here, nor here;
  Nor what ensues but have a fog in them
  That I cannot look through. Away, I prithee,
  Do as I bid thee: There's no more to say:
  Accessible is none but Milford way.

                              Exeunt.

III. 3

Enter Belarius, Guiderius, and Arviragus.

BELARIUS: A goodly day, not to keep house with such,
  Whose roof's as low as ours: Sleep Boys, this gate
  Instructs you now t'adore the Heavens; and bows you
  To a morning's holy office. The gates of Monarchs
  Are arch'd so high, that Giants may jet through
  And keep their impious turbonds on, without
  Good morrow to the Sun. Hail thou fair Heaven,
  We house i'th'rock, yet use thee not so hardly
  As prouder livers do.

GUIDERIUS: Hail Heaven.

ARVIRAGUS: Hail Heaven.

BELARIUS: Now for our mountain sport, up to yond hill
  Your legs are young: I'll tread these flats. Consider,
  When you above perceive me like a crow,
  That it is place, which lessens, and sets off,
  And you may then revolve what tales, I have told you,
  Of Courts, of Princes; of the tricks in War.
  This service is not service; so being done,
  But being so allowed. To apprehend thus,
  Draws us a profit from all things we see:
  And often to our comfort, shall we find
  The sharded beetle, in a safer hold
  Than is the full-wing'd eagle. Oh this life,
  Is nobler, than attending for a check:
  Richer, than doing nothing for a babe:
  Prouder, than rustling in unpaid-for silk:
  Such gain the cap of him, that makes him fine,
  Yet keeps his book uncross'd: no life to ours.

GUIDERIUS: Out of your proof you speak: we poor
    unfledg'd
  Have never wing'd from view o'th'nest; nor knows not
  What air's from home. Haply this life is best,
  (If quiet life be best) sweeter to you
  That have a sharper known. Well corresponding
  With your stiff age; but unto us, it is
  A cell of ignorance: travailing a bed,
  A prison, or a debtor, that not dares
  To stride a limit.

ARVIRAGUS: What should we speak of
  When we are old as you? When we shall hear
  The rain and wind beat dark December? How
  In this our pinching Cave, shall we discourse
  The freezing hours away? We have seen nothing:
  We are beastly; subtle as the fox for prey,
  Like warlike as the wolf, for what we eat:

Our valour is to chase what flies: Our cage
We make a choir, as doth the prison'd bird,
And sing our bondage freely.

BELARIUS: How you speak.
Did you but know the City's usuries,
And felt them knowingly: the Art o'th'Court,
As hard to leave, as keep: whose top to climb
Is certain falling: or so slipp'ry, that
The fear's as bad as falling. The toil o'th'War,
A pain that only seems to seek out danger
I' th' name of Fame, and Honour, which dies i'th'
     search,
And hath as oft a sland'rous epitaph,
As record of fair act. Nay, many times
Doth ill deserve, by doing well: what's worse
Must curt'sy at the censure. Oh Boys, this story
The World may read in me: My body's mark'd
With Roman swords; and my report, was once
First, with the best of Note. Cymbeline lov'd me,
And when a Soldier was the theme, my name
Was not far off: then was I as a tree
Whose boughs did bend with fruit. But in one night,
A storm, or robbery (call it what you will)
Shook down my mellow hangings: nay my leaves,
And left me bare to weather.

GUIDERIUS: Uncertain favour.

BELARIUS: My fault being nothing (as I have told you
     oft)
But two Villains, whose false oaths prevail'd
Before my perfect honour, swore to Cymbeline,
I was confederate with the Romans: so
Followed my banishment, and this twenty years,
This rock, and these demesnes, have been my World.
Where I have liv'd at honest freedom, paid
More pious debts to Heaven, than in all

The fore-end of my time. But, up to'th'mountains,
This is not Hunter's language; he that strikes
The venison first, shall be the Lord o'th'Feast,
To him the other two shall minister,
And we will fear no poison, which attends
In place of greater State:
I'll meet you in the valleys.

      Exeunt Guiderius and Arviragus.

How hard it is to hide the sparks of Nature?
These Boys know little they are Sons to'th'King,
Nor Cymbeline dreams that they are alive.
They think they are mine,
And though train'd up thus meanly
I'th'cave, whereon the bow their thoughts do hit,
The roofs of Palaces and Nature prompts them
In simple and low things, to prince it, much
Beyond the trick of others. This Paladour,
The heir of Cymbeline and Britain, who
The King his Father, call'd Guiderius. Jove,
When on my three-foot stool I sit, and tell
The warlike feats I have done, his spirits fly out
Into my story: say thus mine enemy fell,
And thus I set my foot on's neck, even then
The princely blood flows in his cheek, he sweats,
Strains his young nerves, and puts himself in posture
That acts my words. The younger Brother Cadwall,
Once Arviragus, in as like a figure
Strikes life into my speech, and shows much more
His own convincing. Hark, the game is rous'd,
Oh Cymbeline, Heaven and my conscience knows
Thou did'st unjustly banish me: whereon
At three, and two years old, I stole these Babes,
Thinking to bar thee of succession, as
Thou refts me of my Lands. Euriphile,
Thou wast their Nurse, they took thee for their mother,

And every day do honour to her grave:
Myself Belarius, that am Morgan call'd
They take for natural father. The game is up.

Exit.

III.4

Enter Pisanio, and Imogen.

IMOGEN: Thou told'st me when we came from horse, the
    place
Was near at hand: Ne'er long'd my Mother so
To see me first, as I have now. Pisanio, Man:
Where is Posthumus? What is in thy mind
That makes thee stare thus? Wherefore breaks that sigh
From th'inward of thee? One, but painted thus
Would be interpreted a thing perplex'd
Beyond self-explication. Put thyself
Into a haviour of less fear, ere wildness
Vanquish my staider senses. What's the matter?
Why tender'st thou that paper to me, with
A look untender? If't be summer news
Smile to't before: if winterly, thou need'st
But keep that count'nance still. My Husband's hand?
That drug-damn'd Italy, hath out-craftied him,
And he's at some hard point. Speak man, thy tongue
May take off some extremity, which to read
Would be even mortal to me.

PISANIO: Please you read,
And you shall find me (wretched man) a thing
The most disdain'd of Fortune.

Imogen reads.

Thy Mistress (Pisanio) hath played the Strumpet in my bed:
the testimonies whereof, lies bleeding in me. I speak not out of
weak surmises, but from proof as strong as my grief, and as
certain as I expect my revenge. That part, thou (Pisanio)

*must act for me, if thy faith be not tainted with the breach of
hers; let thine own hands take away her life: I shall give
thee opportunity at Milford Haven. She hath my letter for the
purpose; where, if thou fear to strike, and to make me
certain it is done, thou art the Pandar to her dishonour, and
equally to me disloyal.*

PISANIO: What shall I need to draw my sword, the paper
Hath cut her throat already? No, 'tis Slander,
Whose edge is sharper than the Sword, whose tongue
Out-venoms all the worms of Nile, whose breath
Rides on the posting winds, and doth belie
All corners of the World. Kings, Queens, and States,
Maids, Matrons, nay the Secrets of the Grave
This viperous slander enters. What cheer, Madam?

IMOGEN: False to his bed? What is it to be false?
To lie in watch there, and to think on him?
To weep 'twixt clock and clock? If sleep charge Nature,
To break it with a fearful dream of him,
And cry myself awake? That's false to's bed? Is it?

PISANIO: Alas good Lady.

IMOGEN: I false? Thy conscience witness: Iachimo,
Thou did'st accuse him of incontinency,
Thou then look'dst like a villain: now, methinks
Thy favour's good enough. Some Jay of Italy
(Whose mother was her painting) hath betray'd him:
Poor I am stale, a garment out of fashion,
And for I am richer than to hang by th'walls.
I must be ripp'd: To pieces with me: Oh!
Men's vows are women's traitors. All good seeming
By thy revolt (oh Husband) shall be thought
Put on for villainy; not born where't grows,
But worn a bait for Ladies.

PISANIO: Good Madam, hear me.

IMOGEN: True honest men being heard, like false Aeneas,
Were in his time thought false: and Sinon's weeping

Did scandal many a holy tear: took pity
From most true wretchedness. So thou, Posthumus
Wilt lay the leaven on all proper men;
Goodly, and gallant, shall be false and perjur'd
From thy great fail: Come Fellow, be thou honest,
Do thou thy Master's bidding. When thou seest him,
A little witness my obedience. Look
I draw the sword myself, take it, and hit
The innocent mansion of my Love (my Heart:)
Fear not, 'tis empty of all things, but grief:
Thy Master is not there, who was indeed
The riches of it. Do his bidding, strike,
Thou mayst be valiant in a better cause;
But now thou seem'st a coward.

PISANIO: Hence vile instrument,
Thou shalt not damn my hand.

IMOGEN: Why, I must die:
And if I do not by thy hand, thou art
No servant of thy Master's. Against self-slaughter,
There is a prohibition so divine,
That cravens my weak hand: Come, here's my heart:
Something's a-foot: Soft, soft, we'll no defence,
Obedient as the scabbard. What is here,
The Scriptures of the loyal Leonatus,
All turn'd to Heresy? Away, away
Corrupters of my Faith, you shall no more
Be stomachers to my heart: thus may poor Fools
Believe false Teachers: Though those that are betray'd
Do feel the Treason sharply, yet the Traitor
Stands in worse case of woe. And thou Posthumus,
That did'st set up my disobedience 'gainst the King
My Father, and makes me put into contempt the suits
Of princely fellows, shalt hereafter find
It is no act of common passage, but
A strain of rareness: and I grieve myself,

To think, when thou shalt be disedg'd by her,
That now thou tirest on, how thy memory
Will then be pang'd by me. Prithee dispatch,
The Lamb entreats the Butcher. Where's thy knife?
Thou art too slow to do thy Master's bidding
When I desire it too.

PISANIO: Oh gracious Lady:
Since I receiv'd command to do this business,
I have not slept one wink.

IMOGEN: Do't, and to bed then.

PISANIO: I'll wake mine eye-balls first.

IMOGEN: Wherefore then
Did'st undertake it? Why hast thou abus'd
So many miles, with a pretence? This place?
Mine action? and thine own? Our horses' labour?
The time inviting thee? The perturb'd Court
For my being absent? whereunto I never
Purpose return. Why hast thou gone so far
To be unbent? when thou hast ta'en thy stand,
Th'elected deer before thee?

PISANIO: But to win time
To lose so bad employment, in the which
I have consider'd of a course: good Lady
Hear me with patience.

IMOGEN: Talk thy tongue weary, speak:
I have heard I am a Strumpet, and mine ear
Therein false struck, can take no greater wound,
Nor tent, to bottom that. But speak.

PISANIO: Then Madam,
I thought you would not back again.

IMOGEN: Most like,
Bringing me here to kill me.

PISANIO: Not so neither:
But if I were as wise, as honest, then
My purpose would prove well: it cannot be,

But that my Master is abus'd. Some Villain,
Ay, and singular in his Art, hath done you both
This cursed injury.
IMOGEN: Some Roman Courtesan?
PISANIO: No, on my life:
  I'll give but notice you are dead, and send him
  Some bloody sign of it. For 'tis commanded
  I should do so: you shall be miss'd at Court,
  And that will well confirm it.
IMOGEN: Why good fellow,
  What shall I do the while? Where bide? How live?
  Or in my life, what comfort, when I am
  Dead to my Husband?
PISANIO: If you'll back to'th'Court.
IMOGEN: No Court, no Father, nor no more ado
  With that harsh, noble, simple nothing:
  That Cloten, whose love-suit hath been to me
  As fearful as a siege.
PISANIO: If not at Court,
  Then not in Britain must you bide.
IMOGEN: Where then?
  Hath Britain all the Sun that shines? Day? Night?
  Are they not but in Britain? I'th'world's Volume
  Our Britain seems as of it, but not in't:
  In a great pool, a swan's-nest, prithee think
  There's livers out of Britain.
PISANIO: I am most glad
  You think of other place: Th'Ambassador,
  Lucius the Roman comes to Milford-Haven
  Tomorrow. Now, if you could wear a mind
  Dark, as your Fortune is, and but disguise
  That which t'appear itself, must not yet be,
  But by self-danger, you should tread a course
  Pretty, and full of view: yea, happily, near
  The residence of Posthumus; so nigh (at least)

That though his actions were not visible, yet
Report should render him hourly to your ear,
As truly as he moves.

IMOGEN: Oh for such means,
Though peril to my modesty, not death on't
I would adventure.

PISANIO: Well then, here's the point:
You must forget to be a woman: change
Command, into obedience. Fear, and niceness
(The handmaids of all women, or more truly
Woman it pretty self) into a waggish courage,
Ready in gibes, quick-answer'd, saucy, and
As quarrelous as the weasel: Nay, you must
Forget that rarest treasure of your cheek,
Exposing it (but oh the harder heart,
Alack no remedy) to the greedy touch
Of common-kissing Titan, and forget
Your laboursome and dainty trims, wherein
You made great Juno angry.

IMOGEN: Nay be brief?
I see into thy end, and am almost
A man already.

PISANIO: First, make yourself but like one.
Fore-thinking this, I have already fit
('Tis in my cloak-bag) doublet, hat, hose, all
That answer to them: Would you in their serving,
(And with what imitation you can borrow
From youth of such a season) 'fore noble Lucius
Present yourself, desire his service: tell him
Wherein you're happy; which will make him know,
If that his head have ear in music, doubtless
With joy he will embrace you: for he's honourable,
And doubling that, most holy. Your means abroad:
You have me rich, and I will never fail
Beginning, nor supplyment.

IMOGEN: Thou art all the comfort
  The Gods will diet me with. Prithee away,
  There's more to be consider'd: but we'll even
  All that good time will give us. This attempt,
  I am soldier too, and will abide it with
  A Prince's courage. Away, I prithee.
PISANIO: Well, Madam, we must take a short farewell,
  Lest being miss'd, I be suspected of
  Your carriage from the Court. My noble Mistress,
  Here is a box, I had it from the Queen,
  What's in't is precious: If you are sick at sea,
  Or stomach-qualm'd at land, a dram of this
  Will drive away distemper. To some shade,
  And fit you to your manhood: may the Gods
  Direct you to the best.
IMOGEN: Amen: I thank thee.

Exeunt.

III. 5

Enter Cymbeline, Queen, Cloten, Lucius,
and Lords.

CYMBELINE: Thus far, and so farewell.
LUCIUS: Thanks, Royal Sir:
  My Emperor hath wrote, I must from hence,
  And am right sorry, that I must report ye
  My Master's Enemy.
CYMBELINE: Our subjects (Sir)
  Will not endure his yoke; and for ourself
  To show less sovereignty than they, must needs
  Appear un-kinglike.
LUCIUS: So Sir: I desire of you
  A conduct over land, to Milford-Haven.
  Madam, all joy befall your Grace, and you.
CYMBELINE: My Lords, you are appointed for that office:

The due of honour, in no point omit:
So farewell noble Lucius.

LUCIUS: Your hand, my Lord.

CLOTEN: Receive it friendly: but from this time forth
I wear it as your Enemy.

LUCIUS: Sir, the event
Is yet to name the winner. Fare you well.

CYMBELINE: Leave not the worthy Lucius, good my Lords
Till he have cross'd the Severn. Happiness.

Exit Lucius, &c.

QUEEN: He goes hence frowning: but it honours us
That we have given him cause.

CLOTEN: 'Tis all the better,
Your valiant Britains have their wishes in it.

CYMBELINE: Lucius hath wrote already to the Emperor
How it goes here. It fits us therefore ripely
Our chariots, and our horsemen be in readiness:
The powers that he already hath in Gallia
Will soon be drawn to head, from whence he moves
His war for Britain.

QUEEN: 'Tis not sleepy business,
But must be look'd to speedily, and strongly.

CYMBELINE: Our expectation that it would be thus
Hath made us forward. But my gentle Queen,
Where is our Daughter? She hath not appear'd
Before the Roman, nor to us hath tender'd
The duty of the day. She look'd us like
A thing more made of malice, than of duty,
We have noted it. Call her before us, for
We have been too slight in sufferance.

QUEEN: Royal Sir,
Since the exile of Posthumus, most retir'd
Hath her life been: the cure whereof, my Lord,
'Tis time must do. Beseech your Majesty,
Forbear sharp speeches to her. She's a Lady

So tender of rebukes, that words are strokes,
And strokes death to her.

Enter a Messenger.

CYMBELINE: Where is she Sir? How
Can her contempt be answer'd?

MESSENGER: Please you Sir,
Her chambers are all lock'd, and there's no answer
That will be given to 'th' loud of noise, we make.

QUEEN: My Lord, when last I went to visit her,
She pray'd me to excuse her keeping close,
Whereto constrain'd by her infirmity,
She should that duty leave unpaid to you
Which daily she was bound to proffer: this
She wish'd me to make known: but our great Court
Made me to blame in memory.

CYMBELINE: Her doors lock'd?
Not seen of late? Grant Heavens, that which I
Fear, prove false.

Exit.

QUEEN: Son, I say, follow the King.

CLOTEN: That man of hers, Pisanio, her old Servant
I have not seen these two days.

Exit.

QUEEN: Go, look after:
Pisanio, thou that stand'st so for Posthumus,
He hath a drug of mine: I pray, his absence
Proceed by swallowing that. For he believes
It is a thing most precious. But for her,
Where is she gone? Haply despair hath seiz'd her:
Or wing'd with fervour of her love, she's flown
To her desir'd Posthumus: gone she is,
To death, or to dishonour, and my end
Can make good use of either. She being down,
I have the placing of the British Crown.

Enter Cloten.

How now, my Son?

CLOTEN: 'Tis certain she is fled:
 Go in and cheer the King, he rages, none
 Dare come about him.

QUEEN: All the better: may
 This night forestall him of the coming day.

Exit Queen.

CLOTEN: I love, and hate her: for she's fair and royal,
 And that she hath all courtly parts more exquisite
 Than Lady, Ladies, Woman, from every one
 The best she hath, and she of all compounded
 Out-sells them all. I love her therefore, but
 Disdaining me, and throwing favours on
 The low Posthumus, slanders so her judgement,
 That what's else rare, is chok'd: and in that point
 I will conclude to hate her, nay indeed,
 To be reveng'd upon her. For, when Fools shall—

Enter Pisanio.

Who is here? What, are you packing sirrah?
 Come hither: Ah you precious Pandar, Villain,
 Where is thy Lady? In a word, or else
 Thou art straightway with the Fiends.

PISANIO: Oh, good my Lord.

CLOTEN: Where is thy Lady? Or by Jupiter,
 I will not ask again. Close Villain,
 I'll have this secret from thy heart, or rip
 Thy heart to find it. Is she with Posthumus?
 From whose so many weights of baseness, cannot
 A dram of worth be drawn.

PISANIO: Alas, my Lord,
 How can she be with him? When was she miss'd?
 He is in Rome.

CLOTEN: Where is she Sir? Come nearer:
 No farther halting: satisfy me home,
 What is become of her?

PISANIO: Oh, my all-worthy Lord.

CLOTEN: All-worthy Villain,
Discover where thy Mistress is, at once,
At the next word: no more of worthy Lord:
Speak, or thy silence on the instant, is
Thy condemnation, and thy death.

PISANIO: Then Sir:
This paper is the history of my knowledge
Touching her flight.

CLOTEN: Let's see't: I will pursue her
Even to Augustus' Throne.

PISANIO: Or this, or perish.
She's far enough, and what he learns by this,
May prove his travel, not her danger.

CLOTEN: Humh.

PISANIO: I'll write to my Lord she's dead: Oh Imogen,
Safe mayst thou wander, safe return again.

CLOTEN: Sirrah, is this letter true?

PISANIO: Sir, as I think.

CLOTEN: It is Posthumus' hand, I know't. Sirrah, if thou
would'st not be a Villain, but do me true service: undergo those employments wherein I should have cause to
use thee with a serious industry, that is, what villainy
soe'er I bid thee do to perform it, directly and truly, I
would think thee an honest man: thou should'st neither
want my means for thy relief, nor my voice for thy
preferment.

PISANIO: Well, my good Lord.

CLOTEN: Wilt thou serve me? For since patiently and constantly thou hast stuck to the bare fortune of that Beggar
Posthumus thou canst not in the course of gratitude, but
be a diligent follower of mine. Wilt thou serve me?

PISANIO: Sir, I will.

CLOTEN: Give me thy hand, here's my purse. Hast any
of thy late Master's garments in thy possession?

PISANIO: I have (my Lord) at my lodging, the same suit he wore, when he took leave of my Lady and Mistress.

CLOTEN: The first service thou dost me, fetch that suit hither, let it be thy first service, go.

PISANIO: I shall my Lord.

Exit.

CLOTEN: Meet thee at Milford-Haven: (I forgot to ask him one thing, I'll remember't anon:) even there, thou villain Posthumus will I kill thee. I would these garments were come. She said upon a time (the bitterness of it, I now belch from my heart) that she held the very garment of Posthumus, in more respect, than my noble and natural person; together with the adornment of my Qualities. With that suit upon my back will I ravish her: first kill him, and in her eyes; there shall she see my valour, which will then be a torment to her contempt. He on the ground, my speech of insultment ended on his dead body, and when my Lust hath dined (which, as I say, to vex her, I will execute in the clothes that she so prais'd:) to the Court I'll knock her back, foot her home again. She hath despis'd me rejoicingly, and I'll be merry in my Revenge.

Enter Pisanio.

Be those the garments?

PISANIO: Ay, my Noble Lord.

CLOTEN: How long is't since she went to Milford-Haven?

PISANIO: She can scarce be there yet.

CLOTEN: Bring this apparel to my chamber, that is the second thing that I have commanded thee. The third is, that thou wilt be a voluntary mute to my design. Be but duteous, and true preferment shall tender itself to thee. My Revenge is now at Milford, would I had wings to follow it. Come, and be true.

Exit.

PISANIO: Thou bid'st me to my loss: for true to thee,
  Were to prove false, which I will never be
  To him that is most true. To Milford go,
  And find not her, whom thou pursuest. Flow, flow
  You heavenly blessings on her: This Fool's speed
  Be cross'd with slowness; Labour be his meed.

Exit.

III.6

Enter Imogen alone.

IMOGEN: I see a man's life is a tedious one,
  I have tir'd myself: and for two nights together
  Have made the ground my bed. I should be sick,
  But that my resolution helps me: Milford,
  When from the mountain top, Pisanio show'd thee,
  Thou wast within a ken. Oh Jove, I think
  Foundations fly the wretched: such I mean,
  Where they should be reliev'd. Two beggars told me,
  I could not miss my way. Will poor folks lie
  That have afflictions on them, knowing 'tis
  A punishment, or trial? Yes; no wonder,
  When rich ones scarce tell true. To lapse in fullness
  Is sorer, than to lie for need: and falsehood
  Is worse in Kings, than beggars. My dear Lord,
  Thou art one o'th'false ones: Now I think on thee,
  My hunger's gone: but even before, I was
  At point to sink, for food. But what is this?
  Here is a path to't: 'tis some savage hold:
  I were best not call; I dare not call: yet Famine
  Ere clean it o're-throw Nature, makes it valiant.
  Plenty, and Peace breeds cowards: Hardness ever
  Of hardiness is mother. Hoa? who's here?
  If anything that's civil, speak: if savage,
  Take, or lend. Hoa? No answer? Then I'll enter.

Best draw my sword; and if mine Enemy
But fear the sword like me, he'll scarcely look on't.
Such a foe, good Heavens.

Exit.

III. 7

Enter Belarius, Guiderius, and Arviragus.

BELARIUS: You Polidore have prov'd best woodman, and
Are Master of the Feast: Cadwall, and I
Will play the cook, and servant, 'tis our match:
The seat of industry would dry, and die
But for the end it works to. Come, our stomachs
Will make what's homely, savoury: Weariness
Can snore upon the flint, when resty Sloth
Finds the down-pillow hard. Now peace be here,
Poor house, that keep'st thyself.

GUIDERIUS: I am throughly weary.

ARVIRAGUS: I am weak with toil, yet strong in appetite.

GUIDERIUS: There is cold meat i'th'cave, we'll brouse on
that
Whil'st what we have kill'd, be cook'd.

BELARIUS: Stay, come not in:
But that it eats our victuals, I should think
Here were a Fairy.

GUIDERIUS: What's the matter, Sir?

BELARIUS: By Jupiter an Angel: or if not
An earthly Paragon. Behold Divineness
No elder than a boy.

Enter Imogen.

IMOGEN: Good masters harm me not:
Before I enter'd here, I call'd, and thought
To have begg'd, or bought, what I have took: good troth
I have stolen nought, nor would not, though I had found
Gold strew'd i'th'floor. Here's money for my meat,

I would have left it on the board, so soon
As I had made my meal; and parted
With prayers for the provider.

GUIDERIUS: Money? Youth.

ARVIRAGUS: All gold and silver rather turn to dirt,
As 'tis no better reckon'd, but of those
Who worship dirty Gods.

IMOGEN: I see you're angry:
Know, if you kill me for my fault, I should
Have died, had I not made it.

BELARIUS: Whither bound?

IMOGEN: To Milford-Haven.

BELARIUS: What's your name?

IMOGEN: Fidele Sir: I have a Kinsman, who
Is bound for Italy; he embark'd at Milford,
To whom being going, almost spent with hunger,
I am fallen in this offence.

BELARIUS: Prithee (fair youth)
Think us no churls: nor measure our good minds
By this rude place we live in. Well encounter'd,
'Tis almost night, you shall have better cheer
Ere you depart; and thanks to stay, and eat it:
Boys, bid him welcome.

GUIDERIUS: Were you a woman, youth,
I should woo hard, but be your Groom in honesty:
I bid for you, as I do buy.

ARVIRAGUS: I'll make't my comfort
He is a man, I'll love him as my Brother:
And such a welcome as I'd give to him
(After long absence) such is yours. Most welcome:
Be sprightly, for you fall 'mongst friends.

IMOGEN: 'Mongst friends?
If Brothers: would it had been so, that they
Had been my Father's Sons, then had my prize
Been less, and so more equal ballasting

To thee Posthumus.

BELARIUS: He wrings at some distress.

GUIDERIUS: Would I could free't.

ARVIRAGUS: Or I, what ere it be,
What pain it cost, what danger: Gods!

BELARIUS: Hark Boys.

IMOGEN: Great men
That had a Court no bigger than this cave,
That did attend themselves, and had the virtue
Which their own conscience seal'd them: laying by
That nothing-gift of differing multitudes
Could not out-peer these twain. Pardon me Gods,
I'd change my sex to be companion with them,
Since Leonatus false.

BELARIUS: It shall be so:
Boys we'll go dress our hunt. Fair youth come in;
Discourse is heavy, fasting: when we have supp'd
We'll mannerly demand thee of thy story,
So far as thou wilt speak it.

GUIDERIUS: Pray draw near.

ARVIRAGUS: The night to'th'Owl,
And morn to th'Lark less welcome.

IMOGEN: Thanks Sir.

ARVIRAGUS: I pray draw near.

Exeunt.

III. 8

Enter two Roman Senators, and Tribunes.

I SENATOR: This is the tenor of the Emperor's Writ;
That since the common men are now in action
'Gainst the Pannonians, and Dalmatians,
And that the Legions now in Gaul, are
Full weak to undertake our wars against
The fallen-off Britains, that we do incite

The Gentry to this business. He creates
Lucius Pro-Consul: and to you the Tribunes
For this immediate Levy, he commands
His absolute Commission. Long live Caesar.

TRIBUNE: Is Lucius General of the Forces?

2 SENATOR: Ay.

TRIBUNE: Remaining now in Gallia?

1 SENATOR: With those Legions
Which I have spoke of, whereunto your levy
Must be suppliant: the words of your Commission
Will tie you to the numbers, and the time
Of their dispatch.

TRIBUNE: We will discharge our duty.

Exeunt.

IV.1

Enter Cloten alone.

CLOTEN: I am near to'th'place where they should meet,
if Pisanio have mapp'd it truly. How fit his garments
serve me? Why should his Mistress who was made by
him that made the Tailor, not be fit too? The rather
(saving reverence of the word) for'tis said a woman's
fitness comes by fits; therein I must play the workman,
I dare speak it to myself, for it is not vainglory for a man,
and his glass, to confer in his own chamber; I mean,
the lines of my body are as well drawn as his; no less
young, more strong, not beneath him in fortunes, beyond him in the advantage of the time, above him in
birth, alike conversant in general services, and more remarkable in single oppositions; yet this imperseverant
Thing loves him in my despite. What Mortality is?
Posthumus, thy head (which now is growing upon thy
shoulders) shall within this hour be off, thy Mistress en-
forced, thy garments cut to pieces before thy face: and

all this done, spurn her home to her Father, who may (happily) be a little angry for my so rough usage: but my Mother having power of his testiness, shall turn all into my commendations. My horse is tied up safe, out sword, and to a sore purpose: Fortune put them into my hand: This is the very description of their meeting place and the Fellow dares not deceive me.

Exit.

IV.2

Enter Belarius, Guiderius, Arviragus, and
Imogen from the Cave.

BELARIUS: You are not well: Remain here in the cave,
    We'll come to you after hunting.

ARVIRAGUS: Brother, stay here:
    Are we not Brothers?

IMOGEN: So man and man should be,
    But clay and clay, differs in dignity,
    Whose dust is both alike. I am very sick.

GUIDERIUS: Go you to hunting, I'll abide with him.

IMOGEN: So sick I am not, yet I am not well:
    But not so citizen a wanton, as
    To seem to die, ere sick: So please you, leave me,
    Stick to your journal course: the breach of Custom,
    Is breach of all. I am ill, but your being by me
    Cannot amend me. Society, is no comfort
    To one not sociable: I am not very sick,
    Since I can reason of it: pray you trust me here,
    I'll rob none but myself, and let me die
    Stealing so poorly.

GUIDERIUS: I love thee: I have spoke it,
    How much the quantity, the weight as much,
    As I do love my Father.

BELARIUS: What? How? how?

ARVIRAGUS: If it be sin to say so (Sir) I yoke me
   In my good Brother's fault: I know not why
   I love this youth, and I have heard you say,
   Love's reason's, without reason. The bier at door,
   And a demand who is't shall die, I'd say
   My Father, not this youth.

BELARIUS: Oh noble strain!
   O worthiness of Nature, breed of Greatness!
   "Cowards father cowards, and base things sire base;
   "Nature hath meal, and bran; contempt, and grace.
   I'm not their Father, yet who this should be,
   Doth miracle itself, lov'd before me.
   'Tis the ninth hour o'th'Morn.

ARVIRAGUS: Brother, farewell.

IMOGEN: I wish ye sport.

ARVIRAGUS: You health. – So please you Sir.

IMOGEN: These are kind Creatures.
   Gods, what lies I have heard:
   Our Courtiers say, all's savage, but at Court;
   Experience, oh thou disprov'st report.
   Th'imperious Seas breeds monsters; for the dish,
   Poor tributary rivers, as sweet fish:
   I am sick still, heart-sick; Pisanio,
   I'll now taste of thy drug.

GUIDERIUS: I could not stir him:
   He said he was gentle, but unfortunate;
   Dishonestly afflicted, but yet honest.

ARVIRAGUS: Thus did he answer me: yet said hereafter,
   I might know more.

BELARIUS: To'th'field, to'th'field:
   We'll leave you for this time, go in, and rest.

ARVIRAGUS: We'll not be long away.

BELARIUS: Pray be not sick,
   For you must be our housewife.

IMOGEN: Well, or ill,

I am bound to you.   *Exit.*

BELARIUS: And shal't be ever.
  This youth, how e'er distress'd, appears he hath had
  Good Ancestors.

ARVIRAGUS: How angel-like he sings?

GUIDERIUS: But his neat cookery?
  He cut our roots in characters,
  And sauc'd our broths, as Juno had been sick.
  And he her dieter.

ARVIRAGUS: Nobly he yokes
  A smiling, with a sigh; as if the sigh
  Was that it was, for not being such a smile:
  The smile, mocking the sigh, that it would fly
  From so divine a temple, to commix
  With winds, that sailors rail at.

GUIDERIUS: I do note,
  That grief and patience rooted in them both,
  Mingle their spurs together.

ARVIRAGUS: Grow patient,
  And let the stinking elder (Grief) untwine
  His perishing root, with the encreasing vine.

BELARIUS: It is great morning. Come away: Who's there?
                    Enter Cloten.

CLOTEN: I cannot find those runagates, that Villain
  Hath mock'd me. I am faint.

BELARIUS: Those runagates?
  Means he not us? I partly know him, 'tis
  Cloten, the Son o'th'Queen. I fear some ambush
  I saw him not these many years, and yet
  I know 'tis he: We are held as outlaws: Hence.

GUIDERIUS: He is but one: you, and my Brother search
  What companies are near: pray you away,
  Let me alone with him.
                    Exeunt Belarius and Arviragus.

CLOTEN: Soft, what are you

That fly me thus? Some villain-mountainers?
I have heard of such. What slave art thou?

GUIDERIUS: A thing
More slavish did I ne'er, than answering
A slave without a knock.

CLOTEN: Thou art a robber,
A law-breaker, a villain: yield thee thief.

GUIDERIUS: To who? to thee? What art thou? Have not I
An arm as big as thine? A heart, as big?
Thy words I grant are bigger: for I wear not
My dagger in my mouth. Say what thou art:
Why I should yield to thee?

CLOTEN: Thou villain base,
Know'st me not by my clothes?

GUIDERIUS: No, nor thy Tailor, Rascal:
Who is thy Grandfather? He made those clothes,
Which (as it seems) make thee.

CLOTEN: Thou precious varlet,
My Tailor made them not.

GUIDERIUS: Hence then, and thank
The man that gave them thee. Thou art some Fool,
I am loath to beat thee.

CLOTEN: Thou injurious Thief,
Hear but my name, and tremble.

GUIDERIUS: What's thy name?

CLOTEN: Cloten, thou villain.

GUIDERIUS: Cloten, thou double villain be thy name,
I cannot tremble at it, were it Toad, or Adder, Spider,
'T would move me sooner.

CLOTEN: To thy further fear,
Nay, to thy mere confusion, thou shalt know
I am Son to'th'Queen.

GUIDERIUS: I am sorry for't: not seeming
So worthy as thy birth.

CLOTEN: Art not afear'd?

GUIDERIUS: Those that I reverence, those I fear: the Wise:
  At Fools I laugh: not fear them.

CLOTEN: Die the death:
  When I have slain thee with my proper hand,
  I'll follow those that even now fled hence:
  And on the gates of Lud's-Town set your heads:
  Yield rustic mountaineer.

Fight and Exeunt.
Enter Belarius and Arviragus.

BELARIUS: No company's abroad?

ARVIRAGUS: None in the world; you did mistake him
  sure.

BELARIUS: I cannot tell: Long is it since I saw him,
  But Time hath nothing blurr'd those lines of favour
  Which then he wore: the snatches in his voice,
  And burst of speaking were as his: I am absolute
  'Twas very Cloten.

ARVIRAGUS: In this place we left them;
  I wish my Brother make good time with him,
  You say he is so fell.

BELARIUS: Being scarce made up,
  I mean to man; he had not apprehension
  Of roaring terrors: For defect of judgement
  Is oft the cause of fear.

Enter Guiderius, with Cloten's head.

  But see thy Brother.

GUIDERIUS: This Cloten was a fool, an empty purse,
  There was no money in't: Not Hercules
  Could have knock'd out his brains, for he had none:
  Yet I not doing this, the Fool had born
  My head, as I do his.

BELARIUS: What hast thou done?

GUIDERIUS: I am perfect what: cut off one Cloten's head,
  Son to the Queen (after his own report)
  Who call'd me Traitor, Mountaineer, and swore

With his own single hand he'd take us in,
   Displace our heads, where (thanks the Gods) they grow
   And set them on Lud's-Town.

BELARIUS: We are all undone.

GUIDERIUS: Why, worthy Father, what have we to lose,
   But that he swore to take our lives? the Law
   Protects not us, then why should we be tender,
   To let an arrogant piece of flesh threat us?
   Play Judge, and Executioner, all himself?
   For we do fear the Law. What company
   Discover you abroad?

BELARIUS: No single soul
   Can we set eye on: but in all safe reason
   He must have some attendants. Though his honour
   Was nothing but mutation, ay, and that
   From one bad thing to worse: Not Frenzy,
   Not absolute madness could so far have rav'd
   To bring him here alone: although perhaps
   It may be heard at Court, that such as we
   Cave here, hunt here, are out-laws, and in time
   May make some stronger head, the which he hearing,
   (As it is like him) might break out, and swear
   He'd fetch us in, yet is't not probable
   To come alone, either he so undertaking,
   Or they so suffering: then on good ground we fear,
   If we do fear this body hath a tail
   More perilous than the head.

ARVIRAGUS: Let Ord'nance
   Come as the Gods fore-say it: howsoe'er,
   My Brother hath done well.

BELARIUS: I had no mind
   To hunt this day: The Boy Fidele's sickness
   Did make my way long forth.

GUIDERIUS: With his own sword,
   Which he did wave against my throat, I have ta'en

D

His head from him: I'll throw't into the creek
Behind our rock, and let it to the sea,
And tell the fishes, he's the Queen's Son, Cloten,
That's all I reak.

Exit.

BELARIUS: I fear 'twill be reveng'd:
Would (Polidore) thou had'st not done't: though valour
Becomes thee well enough.

ARVIRAGUS: Would I had done't:
So the Revenge alone pursu'd me: Polidore
I love thee brotherly, but envy much
Thou hast robb'd me of this deed: I would revenges
That possible strength might meet, would seek us
     through
And put us to our answer.

BELARIUS: Well, 'tis done:
We'll hunt no more today, nor seek for danger
Where there's no profit. I prithee to our rock,
You and Fidele play the cooks: I'll stay
Till hasty Polidore return, and bring him
To dinner presently.

ARVIRAGUS: Poor sick Fidele.
I'll willingly to him, to gain his colour,
I'd let a parish of such Cloten's blood,
And praise myself for charity.

Exit.

BELARIUS: Oh thou Goddess,
Thou divine Nature; thou thyself thou blazon'st
In these two Princely Boys: they are as gentle
As Zephyrs blowing below the violet,
Not wagging his sweet head; and yet, as rough
(Their royal blood enchaf'd) as the rud'st wind,
That by the top doth take the mountain pine,
And make him stoop to th'vale. 'Tis wonder
That an invisible instinct should frame them

To Royalty unlearn'd, Honour untaught,
Civility not seen from other: valour
That wildly grows in them, but yields a crop
As if it had been sow'd: yet still it's strange
What Cloten's being here to us portends,
Or what his death will bring us.

     Enter Guiderius.

GUIDERIUS: Where's my Brother?
I have sent Cloten's clot-pole down the stream,
In embassy to his Mother; his body's hostage
For his return.

     Solemn Music.

BELARIUS: My ingenious instrument,
 (Hark Polidore) it sounds: but what occasion
Hath Cadwall now to give it motion? Hark.

GUIDERIUS: Is he at home?

BELARIUS: He went hence even now.

GUIDERIUS: What does he mean?
Since death of my dear'st Mother
It did not speak before. All solemn things
Should answer solemn accidents. The matter?
Triumphs for nothing, and lamenting toys,
Is jollity for apes, and grief for boys.
Is Cadwall mad?

   Enter Arviragus, with Imogen dead, bearing her
     in his Arms.

BELARIUS: Look, here he comes,
And brings the dire occasion in his arms,
Of what we blame him for.

ARVIRAGUS: The bird is dead
That we have made so much on. I had rather
Have skipp'd from sixteen years of age, to sixty:
To have turn'd my leaping time into a crutch,
Than have seen this.

GUIDERIUS: Oh sweetest, fairest Lily:

My Brother wears thee not the one half so well,
As when thou grew'st thyself.

BELARIUS: Oh Melancholy,
Whoever yet could sound thy bottom? Find
The ooze, to show what coast thy sluggish care
Might'st easilest harbour in. Thou blessed thing,
Jove knows what man thou might'st have made: but I
Thou died'st a most rare Boy, of melancholy.
How found you him?

ARVIRAGUS: Stark, as you see:
Thus smiling, as some fly had tickled slumber,
Not as death's dart being laugh'd at; his right cheek
Reposing on a cushion.

GUIDERIUS: Where?

ARVIRAGUS: O'th'floor:
His arms thus leagu'd, I thought he slept, and put
My clouted brogues from off my feet, whose rudeness
Answer'd my steps too loud.

GUIDERIUS: Why, he but sleeps:
If he be gone, he'll make his grave, a bed:
With female Fairies will his Tomb be haunted,
And worms will not come to thee.

ARVIRAGUS: With fairest flowers
Whilst Summer lasts, and I live here, Fidele,
I'll sweeten thy sad grave: thou shalt not lack
The flower that's like thy face: pale primrose, nor
The azur'd hare-bell, like thy veins: no, nor
The leaf of eglantine, whom not to slander,
Out-sweeten'd not thy breath: the raddock would
With charitable bill (Oh bill sore shaming
Those rich-left-heirs, that let their Fathers lie
Without a Monument) bring thee all this,
Yea, and furr'd moss besides. When flowers are none
To winter-ground thy corse –

GUIDERIUS: Prithee have done,

And do not play in wench-like words with that
Which is so serious. Let us bury him,
And not protract with admiration, what
Is now due debt. To'th'grave.

ARVIRAGUS: Say, where shall's lay him?

GUIDERIUS: By good Euriphile, our Mother.

ARVIRAGUS: Be't so:
And let us (Polidore) though now our voices
Have got the mannish crack, sing him to th'ground
As once to our Mother: use like note, and words,
Save that Euriphile, must be Fidele.

GUIDERIUS: Cadwall,
I cannot sing: I'll weep, and word it with thee;
For notes of sorrow, out of tune, are worse
Than Priests, and Fanes that lie.

ARVIRAGUS: We'll speak it then.

BELARIUS: Great griefs I see med'cine the less: For Cloten
Is quite forgot. He was a Queen's Son, Boys,
And though he came our enemy remember
He was paid for that: though mean, and mighty rotting
Together have one dust, yet Reverence
(That Angel of the world) doth make distinction
Of place 'tween high, and low. Our Foe was princely,
And though you took his life, as being our Foe,
Yet bury him, as a Prince.

GUIDERIUS: Pray you fetch him hither,
Thersites' body is as good as Aiax,
When neither are alive.

ARVIRAGUS: If you'll go fetch him,
We'll say our song the whilst: Brother begin.

GUIDERIUS: Nay Cadwall, we must lay his head to'th'
East,
My Father hath a reason for't.

ARVIRAGUS: 'Tis true.

GUIDERIUS: Come on then, and remove him.

ARVIRAGUS: So, begin.

SONG

GUIDERIUS: *Fear no more the heat o'th' Sun,*
              Nor the furious Winter's rages,
              Thou thy worldly task hast done,
              Home art gone, and ta'en thy wages.
              Golden Lads, and Girls all must,
              As Chimney-sweepers come to dust.

ARVIRAGUS: *Fear no more the frown o'th' Great.*
              Thou art past the Tyrant's stroke,
              Care no more to clothe and eat,
              To thee the reed is as the oak:
                  The scepter, learning, physick must,
                  All follow this and come to dust.

GUIDERIUS: *Fear no more the lightning flash.*
ARVIRAGUS: *Nor th'all dreaded thunderstone.*
GUIDERIUS: *Fear not slander, censure rash.*
ARVIRAGUS: *Thou hast finish'd joy and moan.*
BOTH: *All Lovers young, all Lovers must,*
              Consign to thee and come to dust.

GUIDERIUS: *No Exorciser harm thee,*
ARVIRAGUS: *Nor no witch-craft charm thee.*
GUIDERIUS: *Ghost unlaid forbear thee.*
ARVIRAGUS: *Nothing ill come near thee.*
BOTH: *Quiet consummation have,*
              And renowned be thy grave.

Enter Belarius with the body of Cloten.

GUIDERIUS: We have done our obsequies:
    Come lay him down.
BELARIUS: Here's a few flowers, but 'bout midnight
    more:
    The herbs that have on them cold dew o'th'night
    Are strewings fit'st for graves: upon their faces
    You were as flowers, now wither'd: even so

These herblets shall, which we upon you strew.
Come on, away, apart upon our knees:
The ground that gave them first, has them again:
Their pleasures here are past, so are their pain.

Exeunt.

Imogen awakes.

MOGEN: Yes Sir, to Milford-Haven, which is the way?
I thank you: by yond bush? pray how far thither?
'Ods pittikins: can it be six mile yet?
I have gone all night: 'Faith, I'll lie down, and sleep.
But soft; no bedfellow? Oh Gods, and Goddesses!
These flowers are like the pleasures of the World;
This bloody man the care on't. I hope I dream:
For so I thought I was a cave-keeper,
And cook to honest creatures. But 'tis not so:
'Twas but a bolt of nothing, shot at nothing,
Which the brain makes of fumes. Our very eyes,
Are sometimes like our judgements, blind. Good faith
I tremble still with fear: but if there be
Yet left in Heaven, as small a drop of pity
As a wren's eye; fear'd Gods, a part of it.
The dream's here still: even when I wake it is
Without me, as within me: not imagin'd, felt.
A headless man? The garments of Posthumus?
I know the shape of's leg: this is his hand:
His foot Mercurial: his martial thigh
The brawns of Hercules: but his Jovial face —
Murther in heaven? How? 'tis gone. Pisanio,
All curses madded Hecuba gave the Greeks,
And mine to boot, be darted on thee: thou
Conspir'd with that irregulous devil Cloten,
Hath here cut off my Lord. To write, and read,
Be henceforth treacherous. Damn'd Pisanio,
Hath with his forged letters (damn'd Pisanio)
From this most bravest vessel of the world

Struck the main top! Oh Posthumus, alas,
Where is thy head? where's that? Aye me! where's that
Pisanio might have kill'd thee at the heart,
And left this head on. How should this be, Pisanio?
'Tis he, and Cloten: Malice, and Lucre in them
Have laid this woe here. Oh 'tis pregnant, pregnant!
The drug he gave me, which he said was precious
And cordial to me, have I not found it
Murd'rous to'th' senses? That confirms it home:
This is Pisanio's deed, and Cloten: Oh!
Give colour to my pale cheek with thy blood,
That we the horrider may seem to those
Which chance to find us. Oh, my Lord! my Lord!
    Enter Lucius, Captains, and a Soothsayer.

CAPTAIN: To them, the Legions garrison'd in Gallia
  After your will, have cross'd the Sea, attending
  You here at Milford-Haven, with your ships:
  They are here in readiness.

LUCIUS: But what from Rome?

CAPTAIN: The Senate hath stirr'd up the confiners,
  And Gentlemen of Italy, most willing spirits,
  That promise noble service: and they come
  Under the conduct of bold Iachimo,
  Sienna's Brother.

LUCIUS: When expect you them?

CAPTAIN: With the next benefit o'th'wind.

LUCIUS: This forwardness
  Makes our hopes fair. Command our present numbers
  Be muster'd: bid the Captains look to't. Now Sir,
  What have you dream'd of late of this war's purpose.

SOOTHSAYER: Last night, the very Gods show'd me a vision
  (I fast, and pray'd for their intelligence) thus:
  I saw Jove's Bird, the Roman Eagle wing'd
  From the spungy South, to this part of the West,

There vanish'd in the sunbeams, which portends
(Unless my sins abuse my Divination)
Success to th'Roman host.

LUCIUS: Dream often so,
And never false. Soft hoa, what trunk is here?
Without his top? The ruin speaks, that sometime
It was a worthy building. How? a Page?
Or dead, or sleeping on him? But dead rather:
For Nature doth abhor to make his bed
With the defunct, or sleep upon the dead.
Let's see the Boy's face.

CAPTAIN: He's alive my Lord.

LUCIUS: He'll then instruct us of this body: Young one,
Inform us of thy fortunes, for it seems
They crave to be demanded: who is this
Thou mak'st thy bloody pillow? or who was he
That (otherwise then noble Nature did)
Hath alter'd that good picture? What's thy interest
In this sad wrack? How came't? Who is't?
What art thou?

IMOGEN: I am nothing; or if not,
Nothing to be were better: This was my Master,
A very valiant Britain, and a good,
That here by Mountaineers lies slain: Alas,
There is no more such Masters: I may wander
From East to Occident, cry out for service,
Try many, all good: serve truly: never
Find such another Master.

LUCIUS: 'Lack, good youth:
Thou mov'st no less with thy complaining, than
Thy Master in bleeding: say his name, good friend.

IMOGEN: Richard du Champ. If I do lie, and do
No harm by it, though the Gods hear, I hope
They'll pardon it. Say you Sir?

LUCIUS: Thy name?

IMOGEN: Fidele Sir.

LUCIUS: Thou dost approve thyself the very same:
Thy name well fits thy faith; thy faith, thy name:
Wilt take thy chance with me? I will not say
Thou shalt be so well master'd, but be sure
No less belov'd. The Roman Emperor's Letters
Sent by a Consul to me, should not sooner
Than thine own worth prefer thee: Go with me.

IMOGEN: I'll follow Sir. But first, and't please the Gods,
I'll hide my Master from the flies, as deep
As these poor pickaxes can dig: and when
With wild wood-leaves and weeds, I ha' strew'd his grave
And on it said a century of prayers
(Such as I can) twice o'er, I'll weep, and sigh,
And leaving so his service, follow you,
So please you entertain me.

LUCIUS: Ay good youth,
And rather father thee, than master thee: My Friends,
The Boy hath taught us manly duties: Let us
Find out the prettiest daisied-plot we can,
And make him with our pikes and partizans
A grave: Come, arm him: Boy he's preferr'd
By thee, to us, and he shall be interr'd
As Soldiers can. Be cheerful; wipe thine eyes,
Some falls are means the happier to arise.

Exeunt.

IV. 3

Enter Cymbeline, Lords, and Pisanio.

CYMBELINE: Again: and bring me word how 'tis with her,
A fever with the absence of her Son;
A madness, of which her life's in danger: Heavens,
How deeply you at once do touch me. Imogen,
The great part of my comfort, gone: My Queen

Upon a desperate bed, and in a time
When fearful Wars point at me: Her Son gone,
So needful for this present? It strikes me, past
The hope of comfort. But for thee, Fellow,
Who needs must know of her departure, and
Dost seem so ignorant, we'll enforce it from thee
By a sharp torture.

PISANIO: Sir, my life is yours,
  I humbly set it at your will: But for my Mistress,
  I nothing know where she remains: why gone,
  Nor when she purposes return. Beseech your Highness,
  Hold me your loyal Servant.

LORD: Good my Liege,
  The day that she was missing, he was here;
  I dare be bound he's true, and shall perform
  All parts of his subjection loyally. For Cloten,
  There wants no diligence in seeking him,
  And will no doubt be found:

CYMBELINE: The time is troublesome:
  We'll slip you for a season, but our jealousy
  Does yet depend.

LORD: So please your Majesty,
  The Roman Legions, all from Gallia drawn,
  Are landed on your coast, with a supply
  Of Roman Gentlemen, by the Senate sent.

CYMBELINE: Now for the counsel of my Son and Queen.
  I am amaz'd with matter.

LORD: Good my Liege,
  Your preparation can affront no less
  Than what you hear of. Come more, for more you're
    ready:
  The want is, but to put those powers in motion,
  That long to move.

CYMBELINE: I thank you: let's withdraw
  And meet the Time, as it seeks us. We fear not

What can from Italy annoy us, but
We grieve at chances here. Away.

Exeunt.

PISANIO: I heard no letter from my Master, since
I wrote him Imogen was slain. 'Tis strange:
Nor hear I from my Mistress, who did promise
To yield me often tidings. Neither know I
What is betide to Cloten, but remain
Perplex'd in all. The Heavens still must work:
Wherein I am false, I am honest: not true, to be true.
These present wars shall find I love my Country,
Even to the note o'th'King, or I'll fall in them:
All other doubts, by time let them be clear'd,
Fortune brings in some boats, that are not steer'd.

Exit.

IV. 4

Enter Belarius, Guiderius, and Arviragus.

GUIDERIUS: The noise is round about us.

BELARIUS: Let us from it.

ARVIRAGUS: What pleasure Sir, we find in life, to lock it
From action, and adventure?

GUIDERIUS: Nay, what hope
Have we in hiding us? This way the Romans
Must, or for Britains slay us or receive us
For barbarous and unnatural revolts
During their use, and slay us after.

BELARIUS: Sons,
We'll higher to the mountains, there secure us.
To the King's party there's no going: newness
Of Cloten's death (we being not known, nor muster'd
Among the Bands) may drive us to a render
Where we have liv'd; and so extort from's that
Which we have done, whose answer would be death

Drawn on with torture.
GUIDERIUS: This is (Sir) a doubt
In such a time, nothing becoming you,
Nor satisfying us.
ARVIRAGUS: It is not likely,
That when they hear their Roman horses neigh,
Behold their quarter'd fires; have both their eyes
And ears so cloy'd importantly as now,
That they will waste their time upon our note,
To know from whence we are.
BELARIUS: Oh, I am known
Of many in the Army: Many years
(Though Cloten then but young) you see, not wore him
From my remembrance. And besides, the King
Hath not deserv'd my service, nor your loves,
Who find in my exile, the want of breeding;
The certainty of this hard life, aye hopeless
To have the courtesy your cradle promis'd,
But to be still hot Summer's tanlings, and
The shrinking slaves of Winter.
GUIDERIUS: Than be so,
Better to cease to be. Pray Sir, to'th'Army:
I, and my Brother are not known; yourself
So out of thought, and thereto so o'er-grown,
Cannot be question'd.
ARVIRAGUS: By this Sun that shines
I'll thither: What thing is't, that I never
Did see man die, scarce ever look'd on blood,
But that of coward hares, hot goats, and venison?
Never bestrid a horse save one, that had
A rider like myself, who ne're wore rowel,
Nor iron on his heel? I am asham'd
To look upon the holy Sun, to have
The benefit of his bless'd beams, remaining
So long a poor unknown.

GUIDERIUS: By heavens I'll go,
  If you will bless me Sir, and give me leave,
  I'll take the better care: but if you will not,
  The hazard therefore due fall on me, by
  The hands of Romans.
ARVIRAGUS: So say I, Amen.
BELARIUS: No reason I (since of your lives you set
  So slight a valuation) should reserve
  My crack'd one to more care. Have with you Boys:
  If in your country wars you chance to die,
  That is my bed too (Lads) and there I'll lie.
  Lead, lead; the time seems long, their blood thinks scorn
  Till it fly out, and show them Princes born.
                    Exeunt.

V. I

Enter Posthumus alone.

POSTHUMUS: Yea bloody cloth, I'll keep thee: for I am
    wish'd
  Thou should'st be colour'd thus. You married ones,
  If each of you should take this course, how many
  Must murther wives much better than themselves
  For wrying but a little? Oh Pisanio,
  Every good Servant does not all commands:
  No bond, but to do just ones. Gods, if you
  Should have ta'en vengeance on my faults, I never
  Had liv'd to put on this: so had you saved
  The noble Imogen, to repent, and struck
  Me (wretch) more worth your vengeance. But alack,
  You snatch some hence for little faults; that's love
  To have them fall no more: you some permit
  To second ills with ills, each elder worse,
  And make them dread it, to the doer's thrift.
  But Imogen is your own, do your best wills,

And make me bless'd to obey. I am brought hither
Among th' Italian Gentry, and to fight
Against my Lady's Kingdom: 'Tis enough
That (Britain) I have kill'd thy Mistress: Peace,
I'll give no wound to thee: therefore good Heavens,
Hear patiently my purpose. I'll disrobe me
Of these Italian weeds, and suit myself
As does a Britain peasant: so I'll fight
Against the part I come with: so I'll die
For thee (O Imogen) even for whom my life
Is every breath, a death: and thus, unknown,
Pitied, nor hated, to the face of peril
Myself I'll dedicate. Let me make men know
More valour in me, than my habits show.
Gods, put the strength o'th'Leonati in me:
To shame the guise o'th'world, I will begin,
The fashion less without, and more within.

Exit.

V.2

Enter Lucius, Iachimo, and the Roman Army at one door:
and the Britain Army at another:
Leonatus Posthumus following like a poor Soldier.
They march over, and go out. Then enter again
in skirmish Iachimo and Posthumus: he vanquisheth
and disarmeth Iachimo, and then leaves him.

IACHIMO: The heaviness and guilt within my bosom,
Takes off my manhood: I have belied a Lady,
The Princess of this Country; and the air on't
Revengingly enfeebles me, or could this carl,
A very drudge of Nature's, have subdu'd me
In my profession? Knighthoods, and Honours born
(As I wear mine) are titles but of scorn.
If that thy Gentry (Britain) go before

This lout, as he exceeds our Lords, the odds
Is, that we scarce are men, and you are Gods.

Exit.

The Battle continues, the Britains fly,
Cymbeline is taken: Then enter to his rescue, Belarius,
Guiderius, and Arviragus.

BELARIUS: Stand, stand, we have th'advantage of the
ground,
The lane is guarded: Nothing routs us, but
The villainy of our fears.

GUIDERIUS. ARVIRAGUS: Stand, stand, and fight.

Enter Posthumus, and seconds the Britains. They
rescue Cymbeline, and Exeunt.

Then enter Lucius, Iachimo, and Imogen.

LUCIUS: Away boy from the troops, and save thyself:
For friends kill friends, and the disorder's such
As war were hood-wink'd.

IACHIMO: 'Tis their fresh supplies.

LUCIUS: It is a day turn'd strangely: or betimes
Let's reinforce, or fly.

Exeunt.

V. 3

Enter Posthumus, and a Britain Lord.

LORD: Cam'st thou from where they made the stand?

POSTHUMUS: I did.

Though you it seems come from the fliers?

LORD: I did.

POSTHUMUS: No blame be to you Sir, for all was lost,
But that the Heavens fought: the King himself
Of his wings destitute, the Army broken,
And but the backs of Britains seen; all flying
Through a strait lane, the Enemy full-hearted,
Lolling the tongue with slaught'ring: having work

More plentiful, than tools to do't: struck down
Some mortally, some slightly touch'd, some falling
Merely through fear, that the strait pass was damm'd
With dead men, hurt behind, and cowards living
To die with length'ned shame.

LORD: Where was this lane?

POSTHUMUS: Close by the battle, ditch'd, and wall'd
    with turf,
Which gave advantage to an ancient Soldier
(An honest one I warrant) who deserv'd
So long a breeding, as his white beard came to,
In doing this for's Country. Athwart the lane,
He, with two striplings (Lads more like to run
The country base, than to commit such slaughter,
With faces fit for masks, or rather fairer
Than those for preservation cas'd, or shame)
Made good the passage, cried to those that fled.
Our Britains' hearts die flying, not our men,
To darkness fleet souls that fly backwards; stand,
Or we are Romans, and will give you that
Like beasts, which you shun beastly, and may save
But to look back in frown: Stand, stand. These three,
Three thousand confident, in act as many:
For three performers are the file, when all
The rest do nothing. With this word stand, stand,
Accommodated by the place; more charming
With their own nobleness, which could have turn'd
A distaff, to a lance, gilded pale looks;
Part shame, part spirit renew'd, that some turn'd coward
But by example (Oh a sin in War,
Damn'd in the first beginners) gan to look
The way that they did, and to grin like lions
Upon the pikes o'th'Hunters. Then began
A stop i'th'chaser; a retire: Anon
A rout, confusion thick: forthwith they fly

Chickens, the way which they stoop'd eagles: Slaves
The strides the victors made: and now our cowards
Like fragments in hard voyages became
The life o'th'need: having found the back door open
Of the unguarded hearts: heavens, how they wound,
Some slain before some dying; some their friends
O'er-born i' th' former wave, ten chas'd by one,
Are now each one the slaughter-man of twenty:
Those that would die, or ere resist, are grown
The mortal bugs o'th'field.

LORD: This was strange chance:
A narrow lane, an old man, and two Boys.

POSTHUMUS: Nay, do not wonder at it: you are made
Rather to wonder at the things you hear,
Than to work any. Will you rhyme upon't,
And vent it for a mock'ry? Here is one:
"*Two Boys, an Oldman (twice a Boy) a Lane,*
"*Preserv'd the Britains, was the Romans' bane.*

LORD: Nay, be not angry Sir.

POSTHUMUS: 'Lack, to what end?
Who dares not stand his foe, I'll be his friend:
For if he'll do, as he is made to do,
I know he'll quickly fly my friendship too.
You have put me into rhyme.

LORD: Farewell, you're angry.

Exit.

POSTHUMUS: Still going? This is a Lord: Oh noble misery
To be i'th'field, and ask what news of me:
Today, how many would have given their honours
To have sav'd their carcases? Took heel to do't,
And yet died too. I, in mine own woe charm'd
Could not find death, where I did hear him groan,
Nor feel him where he struck. Being an ugly Monster,
'Tis strange he hides him in fresh cups, soft beds,
Sweet words; or hath moe ministers than we

That draw his knives i'th'War. Well I will find him:
For being now a favourer to the Britain,
No more a Britain, I have resum'd again
The part I came in. Fight I will no more,
But yield me to the veriest hind, that shall
Once touch my shoulder. Great the slaughter is
Here made by'th'Roman; great the answer be
Britains must take. For me, my ransom's death,
On either side I come to spend my breath;
Which neither here I'll keep, nor bear again,
But end it by some means for Imogen.

Enter two Captains, and Soldiers.

1 CAPTAIN: Great Jupiter be prais'd, Lucius is taken,
'Tis thought the old man, and his sons, were Angels.
2 CAPTAIN: There was a fourth man, in a silly habit,
That gave th'affront with them.
1 CAPTAIN: So 'tis reported:
But none of 'em can be found. Stand, who's there?
POSTHUMUS: A Roman,
Who had not now been drooping here, if seconds
Had answer'd him.
2 CAPTAIN: Lay hands on him: a dog,
A leg of Rome shall not return to tell
What crows have peck'd them here: he brags his service
As if he were of note: bring him to'th'King.

Enter Cymbeline, Belarius, Guiderius, Arviragus,
Pisanio, and Roman Captains. The Captains
present Posthumus to Cymbeline, who
delivers him over to a Jailer.

V.4

Enter Posthumus, and Jailers.

1 JAILER: You shall not now be stolen,
You have locks upon you:

So graze, as you find pasture.

2 JAILER: Ay, or a stomach.

POSTHUMUS: Most welcome bondage; for thou art a way
(I think) to liberty: yet am I better
Than one that's sick o'th'gout, since he had rather
Groan so in perpetuity, than be cur'd
By'th'sure Physician, Death; who is the key
T'unbar these locks. My Conscience, thou art fetter'd
More than my shanks, and wrists; you good Gods give me
The penitent instrument to pick that bolt,
Then free for ever. Is't enough I am sorry?
So children temporal fathers do appease;
Gods are more full of mercy. Must I repent,
I cannot do it better than in gyves,
Desir'd, more than constrain'd, to satisfy
If of my freedom 'tis the main part, take
No stricter render of me, than my all.
I know you are more clement than vile men,
Who of their broken debtors take a third,
A sixth, a tenth, letting them thrive again
On their abatement; that's not my desire.
For Imogen's dear life, take mine, and though
'Tis not so dear, yet 'tis a life; you coin'd it,
'Tween man, and man, they weigh not every stamp:
Though light, take pieces for the figure's sake,
(You rather) mine being yours: and so great Powers,
If you will take this audit, take this life,
And cancel these cold bonds. Oh Imogen,
I'll speak to thee in silence.

Solemn Music. Enter (as in an Apparition)
Sicillius Leonatus, Father to Posthumus, an old man,
attired like a warrior, leading in his hand an
ancient Matron (his wife, and Mother to Posthumus)
with Music before them. Then after other Music
follows the two young Leonati (Brothers

to Posthumus) with wounds as they
died in the war. They circle Posthumus round
as he lies sleeping.

SICILLIUS: No more thou Thunder-Master
    show thy spite on Mortal Flies:
With Mars fall out with Juno chide, that thy adulteries
    Rates, and revenges.
Hath my poor Boy done ought but well,
    whose face I never saw:
I died whil'st in the womb he stay'd,
    attending Nature's Law.
Whose Father then (as men report,
    thou Orphans' Father art)
Thou should'st have been, and shielded him,
    from this earth-vexing smart.

MOTHER: Lucina lent not me her aid,
    but took me in my throes,
That from me was Posthumus ripp'd,
    came crying 'mongst his foes.
A thing of pity.

SICILLIUS: Great Nature like his Ancestry,
    moulded the stuff so fair;
That he deserv'd the praise o'th'World,
    as great Sicillius' heir.

1 BROTHER: When once he was mature for man,
    in Britain where was he
That could stand up his parallel?
    Or fruitful object be?
In eye of Imogen, that best could deem
    his dignity.

MOTHER: With marriage wherefore was he mock'd
    to be exil'd, and thrown
From Leonati Seat, and cast from her,
    his dearest one:
Sweet Imogen?

SICILLIUS: Why did you suffer Iachimo, slight thing of
    Italy,
  To taint his nobler heart and brain, with needless jealousy
  And to become the geek and scorn o'th'other's villainy?
2 BROTHER: For this, from stiller seats we came,
    our Parents, and us twain,
  That striking in our Country's cause,
    fell bravely, and were slain,
  Our fealty, and Tenantius' right, with Honour to main-
    tain.
1 BROTHER: Like hardiment Posthumus hath
    to Cymbeline perform'd:
  Then Jupiter, the King of Gods, why hast thou thus
    adjourn'd
  The graces for his merits due, being all to dolours
    turn'd?
SICILLIUS: Thy crystal window ope; look,
    look out, no longer exercise
  Upon a valiant Race, thy harsh, and potent injuries:
MOTHER: Since (Jupiter) our Son is good,
    take off his miseries.
SICILLIUS: Peep through thy marble Mansion, help,
    or we poor Ghosts will cry
  To'th'shining Synod of the rest, against thy Deity.
BROTHERS: Help (Jupiter) or we appeal,
    and from thy justice fly.
      Jupiter descends in Thunder, and Lightning,
      sitting upon an Eagle: he throws a Thunder-bolt.
        The Ghosts fall on their knees.
JUPITER: No more you petty spirits of Region low
  Offend our hearing: hush. How dare you Ghosts
  Accuse the Thunderer, whose bolt (you know)
  Sky-planted, batters all rebelling coasts.
  Poor shadows of Elizium, hence, and rest
  Upon your never-withering banks of flowers.

Be not with mortal accidents oppress'd,
No care of yours it is, you know 'tis ours.
Whom best I love, I cross; to make my gift
The more delay'd, delighted. Be content,
Your low-laid Son, our Godhead will uplift:
Ois comforts thrive, his trials well are spent:
Hur Jovial Star reign'd at his birth, and in
Our Temple was he married: Rise, and fade,
He shall be Lord of Lady Imogen,
And happier much by his affliction made.
This Tablet lay upon his breast, wherein
Our pleasure, his full Fortune, doth confine,
And so away: no farther with your din
Express impatience, lest you stir up mine:
Mount Eagle, to my Palace Crystalline.

Ascends.

SICILLIUS: He came in thunder, his celestial breath
    Was sulphurous to smell: the holy Eagle
    Stoop'd, as to foot us: his Ascension is
    More sweet than our bless'd Fields: his Royal Bird
    Prunes the immortal wing, and cloys his beak,
    As when his God is pleas'd.

ALL: Thanks Jupiter.

SICILLIUS: The Marble Pavement closes, he is enter'd
    His radiant Roof: Away, and to be bless'd
    Let us with care perform his great behest.

Vanish.

POSTHUMUS: Sleep, thou hast been a Grandsire, and begot
    A Father to me: and thou hast created
    A Mother, and two Brothers. But (oh scorn)
    Gone, they went hence so soon as they were born:
    And so I am awake. Poor wretches, that depend
    On Greatness, Favour; Dream as I have done,
    Wake, and find nothing. But (alas) I swerve:
    Many dream not to find, neither deserve,

And yet are steep'd in favours; so am I
That have this golden chance, and know not why:
What Fairies haunt this ground? A Book? Oh rare one,
Be not, as is our fangled world, a garment
Nobler than that it covers. Let thy effects
So follow, to be most unlike our Courtiers,
As good, as promise.

Reads.

When as a Lion's whelp, shall to himself unknown, with-out seeking find, and be embrac'd by a piece of tender Air: And when from a stately Cedar shall be lop't branches, which being dead many years, shall after revive, be jointed to the old Stock, and freshly grow, then shall Posthumus end his miseries, Britain be fortunate, and flourish in Peace and Plenty.

'Tis still a dream; or else such stuff as madmen
Tongue, and brain not: either both, or nothing,
Or senseless speaking, or a speaking such
As sense cannot untie. Be what it is,
The action of my life is like it, which I'll keep
If but for sympathy.

Enter Jailer.

JAILER: Come Sir, are you ready for death?

POSTHUMUS: Over-roasted rather: ready long ago.

JAILER: Hanging is the word, Sir, if you be ready for that, you are well cook'd.

POSTHUMUS: So if I prove a good repast to the spectators, the dish pays the shot.

JAILER: A heavy reckoning for you Sir: But the comfort is you shall be called to no more payments, fear no more tavern bills, which are often the sadness of parting, as the procuring of mirth: you come in faint for want of meat, depart reeling with too much drink: sorry that you have paid too much, and sorry that you are paid too much: purse and brain, both empty: the brain the heavier, for being too light; the purse too light, being drawn of heaviness: Oh, of this contradiction you shall now be quit: Oh the charity of a penny cord, it sums up thousands in a trice: you have no true debitor, and creditor but it: of what's past, is, and to come, the discharge: your neck (Sir) is pen, book, and counters; so the acquittance follows.

POSTHUMUS: I am merrier to die, than thou art to live.

JAILER: Indeed Sir, he that sleeps, feels not the toothache: but a man that were to sleep your sleep, and a hangman to help him to bed, I think he would change places with his officer: for, look you Sir, you know not which way you shall go.

POSTHUMUS: Yes indeed do I, fellow.

JAILER: Your death has eyes in's head then: I have not seen him so pictur'd: you must either be directed by some that take upon them to know, or to take upon yourself that which I am sure you do not know: or jump the after-enquiry on your own peril: and how you shall speed in your journey's end, I think you'll never return to tell one.

POSTHUMUS: I tell thee, fellow, there are none want eyes, to direct them the way I am going, but such as wink, and will not use them.

JAILER: What an infinity mock is this, that a man should have the best use of eyes, to see the way of blindness: I am sure hanging's the way of winking.

Enter a Messenger.

MESSENGER: Knock off his manacles, bring your prisoner to the King.

POSTHUMUS: Thou bring'st good news, I am call'd to be made free.

JAILER: I'll be hang'd then.

POSTHUMUS: Thou shalt be then freer than a Jailer; no bolts for the dead.

JAILER: Unless a man would marry a gallows, and beget
   young gibbets, I never saw one so prone: yet on my
   conscience, there are verier knaves desire to live, for all
   he be a Roman; and there be some of them too that die
   against their wills; so should I, if I were one. I would
   we were all of one mind, and one mind good: O there
   were desolation of jailers and galowses: I speak against
   my present profit, but my wish hath a preferment in't.
   Exeunt.

V. 5

Enter Cymbeline, Belarius, Guiderius,
Arviragus, Pisanio, and Lords.

CYMBELINE: Stand by my side you, whom the Gods have
   made
   Preservers of my Throne: woe is my heart,
   That the poor Soldier that so richly fought,
   Whose rags, sham'd gilded arms, whose naked breast
   Stepp'd before targes of proof, cannot be found:
   He shall be happy that can find him, if
   Our Grace can make him so.

BELARIUS: I never saw
   Such noble fury in so poor a Thing;
   Such precious deeds, in one that promis'd nought
   But beggary, and poor looks.

CYMBELINE: No tidings of him?

PISANIO: He hath been search'd among the dead, and
   living;
   But no trace of him.

CYMBELINE: To my grief, I am
   The heir of his reward, which I will add
   To you (the liver, heart, and brain of Britain)
   By whom (I grant) she lives. 'Tis now the time
   To ask of whence you are. Report it.

BELARIUS: Sir,
  In Cambria are we born, and Gentlemen:
  Further to boast, were neither true, nor modest,
  Unless I add, we are honest.
CYMBELINE: Bow your knees:
  Arise my Knights o'th'Battle, I create you
  Companions to our person, and will fit you
  With dignities becoming your estates.
           Enter Cornelius and Ladies.
  There's business in these faces: why so sadly
  Greet you our victory? you look like Romans,
  And not o' th' Court of Britain.
CORNELIUS: Hail great King,
  To sour your happiness, I must report
  The Queen is dead.
CYMBELINE: Who worse than a Physician
  Would this report become? But I consider
  By med'cine life may be prolong'd, yet death
  Will seize the Doctor too. How ended she?
CORNELIUS: With horror, madly dying, like her life,
  Which (being cruel to the world) concluded
  Most cruel to herself. What she confess'd,
  I will report, so please you. These her Women
  Can trip me, if I err, who with wet cheeks
  Were present when she finish'd.
CYMBELINE: Prithee say.
CORNELIUS: First, she confess'd she never lov'd you: only
  Affected greatness got by you: not you:
  Married your Royalty, was wife to your place:
  Abhorr'd your person.
CYMBELINE: She alone knew this:
  And but she spoke it dying, I would not
  Believe her lips in opening it. Proceed.
CORNELIUS: Your daughter, whom she bore in hand to
   love

With such integrity, she did confess
Was as a scorpion to her sight, whose life
(But that her flight prevented it) she had
Ta'en off by poison.

CYMBELINE: O most delicate Fiend!
Who is't can read a woman? Is there more?

CORNELIUS: More Sir, and worse. She did confess she had
For you a mortal mineral, which being took,
Should by the minute feed on life, and ling'ring,
By inches waste you. In which time, she purpos'd
By watching, weeping, tendance, kissing, to
O'ercome you with her show; and in time
(When she had fitted you with her craft, to work
Her Son into th'adoption of the Crown:
But failing of her end by his strange absence,
Grew shameless desperate, open'd (in despite
Of Heaven and Men) her purposes: repented
The evils she hatch'd, were not effected: so
Despairing, died.

CYMBELINE: Heard you all this, her Women?

LADIES: We did, so please your Highness.

CYMBELINE: Mine eyes
Were not in fault, for she was beautiful:
Mine ears that heard her flattery, nor my heart,
That thought her like her seeming. It had been vicious
To have mistrusted her: yet (Oh my Daughter)
That it was folly in me, thou mayst say,
And prove it in thy feeling. Heaven mend all.

>   *Enter Lucius, Iachimo, and other*
>   *Roman prisoners, Posthumus Leonatus behind,*
>   *and Imogen.*

Thou com'st not Caius now for Tribute, that
The Britains have ras'd out, though with the loss
Of many a bold one: whose kinsmen have made suit
That their good souls may be appeas'd, with slaughter

Of you their captives, which ourself have granted,
So think of your estate.

LUCIUS: Consider Sir, the chance of War, the day
Was yours by accident: had it gone with us,
We should not when the blood was cool, have threaten'd
Our prisoners with the sword. But since the Gods
Will have it thus, that nothing but our lives
May be call'd ransom, let it come: Sufficeth,
A Roman, with a Roman's heart can suffer:
Augustus lives to think on't: and so much
For my peculiar care. This one thing only
I will entreat, my Boy (a Britain born)
Let him be ransom'd: Never Master had
A Page so kind, so duteous, diligent,
So tender over his occasions, true,
So feat, so nurse-like: let his virtue join
With my request, which I'll make bold your Highness
Cannot deny: he hath done no Britain harm,
Though he have serv'd a Roman. Save him (Sir)
And spare no blood beside.

CYMBELINE: I have surely seen him:
His favour is familiar to me: Boy,
Thou hast look'd thyself into my grace,
And art mine own. I know not why, wherefore,
To say, live boy: ne'er thank thy Master, live;
And ask of Cymbeline what boon thou wilt,
Fitting my bounty, and thy state, I'll give it:
Yea, though thou do demand a prisoner
The noblest ta'en.

IMOGEN: I humbly thank your Highness.

LUCIUS: I do not bid thee beg my life, good Lad,
And yet I know thou wilt.

IMOGEN: No, no, alack,
There's other work in hand: I see a thing
Bitter to me, as death: your life, good Master,

Must shuffle for itself.

LUCIUS: The Boy disdains me,
He leaves me, scorns me: briefly die their joys,
That place them on the truth of girls, and boys.
Why stands he so perplex'd?

CYMBELINE: What would'st thou Boy?
I love thee more, and more: think more and more
What's best to ask. Know'st him thou look'st on? Speak
Wilt have him live? Is he thy kin? thy friend?

IMOGEN: He is a Roman, no more kin to me,
Than I to your Highness, who being born your vassal
Am something nearer.

CYMBELINE: Wherefore ey'st him so?

IMOGEN: I'll tell you (Sir) in private, if you please
To give me hearing.

CYMBELINE: Ay, with all my heart.
And lend my best attention. What's thy name?

IMOGEN: Fidele Sir.

CYMBELINE: Thou'rt my good youth: my Page
I'll be thy Master: walk with me: speak freely.

BELARIUS: Is not this Boy reviv'd from death?

ARVIRAGUS: One sand another
Not more resembles that sweet rosy lad:
Who died, and was Fidele: what think you?

GUIDERIUS: The same dead thing alive.

BELARIUS: Peace, peace, see further: he eyes us not, for-
bear.
Creatures may be alike: were't he, I am sure
He would have spoke to us.

GUIDERIUS: But we see him dead.

BELARIUS: Be silent: let's see further.

PISANIO: It is my Mistress:
Since she is living, let the time run on,
To good, or bad.

CYMBELINE: Come, stand thou by our side,

Make thy demand aloud. [*To Iachimo*] Sir, step you
   forth,
Give answer to this Boy, and do it freely,
Or by our Greatness, and the grace of it
(Which is our Honour) bitter torture shall
Winnow the truth from falsehood. One speak to him.

IMOGEN: My boon is that this Gentleman may render
Of whom he had this ring.

POSTHUMUS: What's that to him?

CYMBELINE: That diamond upon your finger, say
How came it yours.

IACHIMO Thou'lt torture me to leave unspoken, that
Which to be spoke, would torture thee.

CYMBELINE: How? me?

IACHIMO: I am glad to be constrain'd to utter that
Which torments me to conceal. By villainy
I got this ring: 'twas Leonatus' jewel,
Whom thou did'st banish: and which more may grieve
   thee,
As it doth me: a nobler Sir, ne'er liv'd
Twixt sky and ground. Wilt thou hear more my Lord?

CYMBELINE: All that belongs to this.

IACHIMO: That Paragon, thy daughter,
For whom my heart drops blood, and my false spirits
Quail to remember. Give me leave, I faint.

CYMBELINE: My Daughter? what of her? Renew thy
   strength
I had rather thou should'st live, while Nature will,
Than die ere I hear more: strive man, and speak.

IACHIMO: Upon a time, unhappy was the clock
That struck the hour: it was in Rome, accurs'd
The mansion where: 'twas at a feast, oh would
Our viands had been poison'd (or at least
Those which I heav'd to head:) the good Posthumus,
(What should I say? he was too good to be

Where ill men were, and was the best of all
Among'st the rar'st of good ones) sitting sadly,
Hearing us praise our Loves of Italy
For beauty, that made barren the swell'd boast
Of him that best could speak: for feature, laming
The Shrine of Venus, or straight-pight Minerva,
Postures, beyond brief Nature. For condition,
A shop of all the qualities, that man
Loves woman for, besides that hook of wiving,
Fairness, which strikes the eye.

CYMBELINE: I stand on fire. Come to the matter.

IACHIMO: All too soon I shall,
Unless thou would'st grieve quickly. This Posthumus,
Most like a noble Lord, in love, and one
That had a Royal Lover, took his hint,
And (not dispraising whom we prais'd, therein
He was as calm as virtue) he began
His Mistress' picture, which, by his tongue, being made,
And then a mind put in't, either our brags
Were crack'd of kitchen-trulls, or his description
Prov'd us unspeaking sots.

CYMBELINE: Nay, nay, to'th'purpose.

IACHIMO: Your daughter's chastity, (there it begins)
He spoke of her, as Dian had hot dreams,
And she alone, were cold: Whereat, I wretch
Made scruple of his praise, and wager'd with him
Pieces of gold, 'gainst this, (which then he wore
Upon his honour'd finger) to attain
In suit the place of's bed, and win this ring
By hers, and mine adultery: he (true Knight)
No lesser of her honour confident
Than I did truly find her, stakes this ring,
And would so, had it been a carbuncle
Of Phoebus' wheel; and might so safely, had it
Been all the worth of's car. Away to Britain

Post I in this design: Well may you (Sir)
Remember me at Court, where I was taught
Of your chaste Daughter, the wide difference
'Twixt amorous, and villainous. Being thus quench'd
Of hope, not longing; mine Italian brain,
Can in your duller Britain operate
Most vilely: for my vantage excellent.
And to be brief, my practise so prevail'd
That I return'd with simular proof enough,
To make the noble Leonatus mad,
By wounding his belief in her renown,
With tokens thus, and thus: averring notes
Of chamber-hanging, pictures, this her bracelet
(Oh cunning how I got) nay some marks
Of secret on her person, that he could not
But think her bond of chastity quite crack'd,
I having ta'en the forfeit. Whereupon,
Me thinks I see him now.

POSTHUMUS: Ay so thou do'st,
Italian Fiend. Aye me, most credulous Fool,
Egregious murtherer, Thief, any thing
That's due to all the Villains past, in being
To come. Oh give me cord, or knife, or poison,
Some upright Justicer. Thou King, send out
For torturers ingenious: it is I
That all th'abhorred things o'th'earth amend
By being worse than they. I am Posthumus,
That kill'd thy Daughter: Villain-like, I lie,
That caus'd a lesser villain than myself,
A sacrilegious Thief to do 't. The Temple
Of Virtue was she; yea, and she herself.
Spit, and throw stones, cast mire upon me, set
The dogs o'th'street to bay me: every villain
Be call'd Posthumus Leonatus, and
Be villainy less than 'twas. Oh Imogen!

E

My Queen, my life, my wife: oh Imogen,
Imogen, Imogen.

IMOGEN: Peace my Lord, hear hear.

POSTHUMUS: Shall's have a play of this?
Thou scornful Page, there lie thy part.

PISANIO: Oh Gentlemen, help,
Mine and your Mistress: Oh my Lord Posthumus,
You ne'er kill'd Imogen till now: help, help,
Mine honour'd Lady.

CYMBELINE: Does the world go round?

POSTHUMUS: How comes these staggers on me?

PISANIO: Wake my Mistress.

CYMBELINE: If this be so, the Gods do mean to strike me
To death, with mortal joy.

PISANIO: How fares my Mistress?

IMOGEN: Oh get thee from my sight,
Thou gav'st me poison: dangerous fellow hence,
Breathe not where Princes are.

CYMBELINE: The tune of Imogen.

PISANIO: Lady, the Gods throw stones of sulphur on me,
if
That box I gave you, was not thought by me
A precious thing, I had it from the Queen.

CYMBELINE: New matter still.

IMOGEN: It poison'd me.

CORNELIUS: Oh Gods!
I left out one thing which the Queen confess'd,
Which must approve thee honest. If Pisanio
Have (said she) given his Mistress that confection
Which I gave him for cordial, she is serv'd,
As I would serve a rat.

CYMBELINE: What's this, Cornelius.

CORNELIUS: The Queen (Sir) very oft importun'd me
To temper poisons for her, still pretending
The satisfaction of her knowledge, only

In killing creatures vile, as cats and dogs
Of no esteem. I dreading, that her purpose
Was of more danger, did compound for her
A certain stuff, which being ta'en, would cease
The present power of life, but in short time,
All offices of Nature, should again
Do their due functions. Have you ta'en of it?

IMOGEN: Most like I did, for I was dead.

BELARIUS: My Boys, there was our error.

GUIDERIUS: This is sure Fidele.

IMOGEN: Why did you throw your wedded Lady fro
    you?
Think that you are upon a rock, and now
Throw me again.

POSTHUMUS: Hang there like fruit, my soul,
Till the tree die.

CYMBELINE: How now, my flesh? my Child?
What, mak'st thou me a dullard in this act?
Wilt thou not speak to me?

IMOGEN: Your blessing, Sir.

BELARIUS: Though you did love this youth, I blame ye
    not,
You had a motive for't.

CYMBELINE: My tears that fall
Prove holy-water on thee; Imogen,
Thy Mother's dead.

IMOGEN: I am sorry for't, my Lord.

CYMBELINE: Oh, she was naught; and long of her it was
That we meet here so strangely: but her Son
Is gone, we know not how, nor where.

PISANIO: My Lord,
Now fear is from me, I'll speak truth. Lord Cloten
Upon my Lady's missing, came to me
With his sword drawn, foam'd at the mouth, and swore
If I discover'd not which way she was gone,

It was my instant death. By accident,
I had a feigned letter of my Master's
Then in my pocket, which directed him
To seek her on the mountains near to Milford,
Where in a frenzy, in my Master's garments
(Which he enforc'd from me) away he posts
With unchaste purpose, and with oath to violate
My Lady's honour, what became of him,
I further know not.

GUIDERIUS: Let me end the story: I slew him there.

CYMBELINE: Marry, the Gods forfend.
I would not thy good deeds, should from my lips
Pluck a hard sentence: Prithee valiant youth
Deny't again.

GUIDERIUS: I have spoke it, and I did it.

CYMBELINE: He was a Prince.

GUIDERIUS: A most uncivil one. The wrongs he did me
Were nothing prince-like; for he did provoke me
With language that would make me spurn the Sea,
If it could so roar to me. I cut off's head,
And am right glad he is not standing here
To tell this tale of mine.

CYMBELINE: I am sorrow for thee:
By thine own tongue thou art condemn'd, and must
Endure our Law: Thou'rt dead.

IMOGEN: That headless man I thought had been my Lord.

CYMBELINE: Bind the offender,
And take him from our presence.

BELARIUS: Stay, Sir King.
This man is better than the man he slew,
As well descended as thyself, and hath
More of thee merited, than a band of Clotens
Had ever scar for. Let his arms alone,
They were not born for bondage.

CYMBELINE: Why old Soldier:

Wilt thou undo the worth thou art unpaid for
By tasting of our wrath? How of descent
As good as we?

ARVIRAGUS: In that he spoke too far.

CYMBELINE: And thou shalt die for't.

BELARIUS: We will die all three,
But I will prove that two on's are as good
As I have given out him. My Sons, I must
For mine own part, unfold a dangerous speech
Though haply well for you.

ARVIRAGUS: Your danger's ours.

GUIDERIUS: And our good his.

BELARIUS: Have at it then, by leave
Thou had'st (great King) a subject, who
Was call'd Belarius.

CYMBELINE: What of him? He is a banish'd Traitor.

BELARIUS: He it is, that hath
Assum'd this age: indeed a banish'd man,
I know not how, a Traitor.

CYMBELINE: Take him hence,
The whole world shall not save him.

BELARIUS: Not too hot;
First pay me for the nursing of thy Sons,
And let it be confiscate all, so soon
As I have receiv'd it.

CYMBELINE: Nursing of my Sons?

BELARIUS: I am too blunt, and saucy: here's my knee:
Ere I arise, I will prefer my Sons,
Than spare not the old Father. Mighty Sir,
These two young Gentlemen that call me Father,
And think they are my Sons, are none of mine,
They are the issue of your loins, my Liege,
And blood of your begetting.

CYMBELINE: How? my Issue.

BELARIUS: So sure as you, your Father's: I (old Morgan)

Am that Belarius, whom you sometime banish'd:
Your pleasure was my near offence, my punishment
Itself, and all my treason that I suffer'd,
Was all the harm I did. These gentle Princes
(For such, and so they are) these twenty years
Have I train'd up; those arts they have, as I
Could put into them. My breeding was (Sir)
As your Highness knows: Their Nurse Euriphile
(Whom for the Theft I wedded) stole these children
Upon my banishment: I mov'd her to't,
Having receiv'd the punishment before
For that which I did then. Beaten for loyalty,
Excited me to treason. Their dear loss,
The more of you 'twas felt, the more it shap'd
Unto my end of stealing them. But gracious Sir,
Here are your Sons again, and I must lose
Two of the sweet'st companions in the World.
The benediction of these covering Heavens
Fall on their heads like dew, for they are worthy
To inlay Heaven with Stars.

CYMBELINE: Thou weep'st, and speak'st:
The service that you three have done, is more
Unlike, than this thou tell'st. I lost my Children,
If these be they, I know not how to wish
A pair of worthier Sons.

BELARIUS: Be pleas'd awhile;
This Gentleman, whom I call Polidore,
Most worthy Prince, as yours, is true Guiderius:
This Gentleman, my Cadwall, Arviragus.
Your younger Princely Son, he Sir, was lapp'd
In a most curious mantle, wrought by th'hand
Of his Queen Mother, which for more probation
I can with ease produce.

CYMBELINE: Guiderius had
Upon his neck a mole, a sanguine star,

It was a mark of wonder.

BELARIUS: That is he,
Who hath upon him still that natural stamp:
It was wise Nature's end, in the donation
To be his evidence now.

CYMBELINE: Oh, what am I
A Mother to the birth of three? Ne'er Mother
Rejoic'd deliverance more: Bless'd, pray you be,
That after this strange starting from your orbs,
You may reign in them now: Oh Imogen,
Thou hast lost by this a Kingdom.

IMOGEN: No, my Lord:
I have got two Worlds by't. Oh my gentle Brothers,
Have we thus met? Oh never say hereafter
But I am truest speaker. You call'd me Brother
When I was but your Sister: I you Brothers,
When we were so indeed.

CYMBELINE: Did you e'er meet?

ARVIRAGUS: Ay my good Lord.

GUIDERIUS: And at first meeting lov'd,
Continued so, until we thought he died.

CORNELIUS: By the Queen's dram she swallow'd.

CYMBELINE: O rare instinct!
When shall I hear all through? This fierce abridgement,
Hath to it circumstantial branches, which
Distinction should be rich in. Where? how liv'd you?
And when came you to serve our Roman Captive?
How parted with your Brother? How first met them?
Why fled you from the Court? And whither these?
And your three motives to the Battle? with
I know not how much more should be demanded,
And all the other by-dependences
From chance to chance? But nor the time, nor place
Will serve our long interrogatories. See,
Posthumus anchors upon Imogen;

And she (like harmless lightning) throws her eye
On him: her Brothers, Me: her Master hitting
Each object with a joy: the counter-change
Is severally in all. Let's quit this ground,
And smoke the Temple with our sacrifices.
Thou art my Brother, so we'll hold thee ever.

IMOGEN: You are my Father too, and did relieve me:
To see this gracious season.

CYMBELINE: All o'er-joy'd
Save these in bonds, let them be joyful too,
For they shall taste our comfort.

IMOGEN: My good Master, I will yet do you service.

LUCIUS: Happy be you.

CYMBELINE: The forlorn Soldier, that so nobly fought
He would have well becom'd this place, and grac'd
The thankings of a King.

POSTHUMUS: I am Sir
The Soldier that did company these three
In poor beseeming: 'twas a fitment for
The purpose I then follow'd. That I was he,
Speak Iachimo, I had you down, and might
Have made you finish.

IACHIMO: I am down again:
But now my heavy conscience sinks my knee,
As then your force did. Take that life, beseech you
Which I so often owe: but your ring first,
And here the bracelet of the truest Princess
That ever swore her faith.

POSTHUMUS: Kneel not to me:
The power that I have on you, is to spare you:
The malice towards you, to forgive you. Live
And deal with others better.

CYMBELINE: Nobly doom'd:
We'll learn our freeness of a Son-in-Law:
Pardon's the word to all.

ARVIRAGUS: You holp us Sir,
  As you did mean indeed to be our Brother,
  Joy'd are we, that you are.
POSTHUMUS: Your Servant Princes, Good my Lord of
    Rome
  Call forth your Sooth-sayer: As I slept, me thought
  Great Jupiter upon his Eagle back'd
  Appear'd to me, with other sprightly shows
  Of mine own kindred. When I wak'd, I found
  This label on my bosom; whose containing
  Is so from sense in hardness, that I can
  Make no collection of it. Let him show
  His skill in the construction.
LUCIUS: Philarmonus.
SOOTHSAYER: Here, my good Lord.
LUCIUS: Read, and declare the meaning.
                    Reads.
When as a Lion's whelp, shall to himself unknown, with-
out seeking find, and be embrac'd by a piece of tender Air:
And when from a stately Cedar shall be lopt branches, which
being dead many years, shall after revive, be jointed to the old
Stock, and freshly grow, then shall Posthumus end his miseries,
Britain be fortunate, and flourish in Peace and Plenty.
  Thou Leonatus art the Lion's Whelp,
  The fit and apt construction of thy name
  Being Leonatus, doth import so much:
  The piece of tender Air, thy virtuous Daughter,
  Which we call *Mollis Aer*, and *Mollis Aer*
  We term it *Mulier*; which *Mulier* I divine
  Is this most constant Wife, who even now
  Answering the letter of the Oracle,
  Unknown to you unsought, were clipp'd about
  With this most tender Air.
CYMBELINE: This hath some seeming.
SOOTHSAYER: The lofty Cedar, Royal Cymbeline

Personates thee: And thy lopt Branches, point
Thy two Sons forth: who by Belarius stolen
For many years thought dead, are now reviv'd
To the Majestic Cedar join'd; whose Issue
Promises Britain, Peace and Plenty.

CYMBELINE: Well,
My peace we will begin: And Caius Lucius,
Although the Victor, we submit to Caesar,
And to the Roman Empire; promising
To pay our wonted Tribute, from the which
We were dissuaded by our wicked Queen,
Whom heavens in Justice both on her, and hers,
Have laid most heavy hand.

SOOTHSAYER: The fingers of the Powers above, do tune
The harmony of this Peace: the Vision
Which I made known to Lucius ere the stroke
Of yet this scarce-cold-battle, at this instant
Is full accomplish'd. For the Roman Eagle
From South to West, on wing soaring aloft
Lessen'd herself, and in the beams o'th'Sun
So vanish'd; which fore-show'd our Princely Eagle
Th'Imperial Caesar, should again unite
His favour, with the Radiant Cymbeline,
Which shines here in the West.

CYMBELINE: Laud we the Gods,
And let our crooked smokes climb to their nostrils
From our bless'd Altars. Publish we this Peace
To all our Subjects. Set we forward: Let
A Roman, and a British Ensign wave
Friendly together: so through Lud's-Town march,
And in the Temple of great Jupiter
Our Peace we'll ratify: Seal it with feasts.
Set on there: Never was a War did cease
(Ere bloody hands were wash'd) with such a Peace
                              Exeunt.

NOTES

References are to the page and line of this edition.
A full page contains 35 lines.

The Actors' Names: *Posthumus*: the name is accented P. 24
on the second syllable – Posthúmus.

Cloten: spelt Clotten for the first half of the Folio P. 24
text, was presumably so pronounced.

Iachimo: as is clear from the passages of verse in P. 24
which it occurs the name is a three-syllable word –
Jachimo.

bloods . . . seem: the passions (*bloods*) of ordinary men P. 25 LL. 4–6
like those of courtiers, go contrary to divine will;
men pretend to be as angry as the King. Editors,
however, usually omit the colon; the sentence then
means 'just as our passions obey the stars (*heavens*),
so our courtiers always (*still*) pretend to be as angry
as the King'.

there . . . compare: anyone chosen for comparison P. 25
cannot help suffering under the test.   LL. 28–9

Endows . . . he: i.e., there is no one endowed with P. 25 L. 31
such outward and inward qualities.

extend . . . himself: exhibit him as he is.   P. 25 L. 33

delve . . . root: trace his ancestry back to its first P. 26 L. 4
origin.

Cassibulan: Cassivellaunus, leader of the resistance P. 26 L. 7
against Julius Caesar's second invasion of Britain in
54 B.C.

had . . . by: won from.   P. 26 L. 8

fond of issue: doting on his children.   P. 26 L. 14

Bedchamber: i.e. in closest personal attendance on the P. 26 L. 19
King. King James's current favourite, Robert Carr,
afterwards Earl of Somerset, began his rapid upward
climb as Groom of the Bedchamber to the King.

spring . . . harvest: was a mature man while yet a P. 26 L. 23
youth.

glass . . . feated: i.e. a standard of comparison that P. 26 L. 26
gave them a sense of security. *feated*: encouraged.

graver . . . dotards: old men find him a guide in their P. 26
second childhood.   LL. 26–7

P. 27 L. 1   *the other:* i.e. the younger also.

P. 27 L. 18   I.2: This scene division is in the Folio. Editors (rightly) do not mark any break in the action.

P. 27 L. 21   *After ... Step-mothers:* according to the ill repute of most stepmothers.

P. 27 L. 28   *lean'd unto:* acquiesced in.

P. 28 L. 22   *gall:* 'oak-apples', a parasitic growth on the oak from which ink was once made.

P. 28   *I ... offences:* whenever I wrong him he always asks
LL. 27–9   for forgiveness, lest we should cease to be friends: he even rewards me for the wrongs that I do him.

P. 29 L. 30   *repair my youth:* make me feel young again by pleasing me.

P. 30 L. 8   *seat for baseness:* i.e. your children by Posthumus
P. 30]   would not have been of pure royal blood.
LL. 14–15   *over-buys ... pays:* i.e. I am worth far less than he.

P. 30 LL. 27–8   *make ... advice:* i.e. take a sensible view of this.

P. 31 L. 11   *in Africk:* i.e. a desert whence there could be no escape.

P. 31 L. 13   *goer back:* loser.

P. 32 LL. 6–7   *steel ... Town:* i.e. his sword did not fulfil its obligations (i.e. he played the coward); it skulked away like a debtor fearing arrest.

P. 32 L. 21   *good sign:* good only in outward appearance.

P. 33 LL. 6–7   *paper ... mercy:* as if the pardon for a condemned man should go astray.

P. 33 L. 15   *could make me:* I could make him out.

P. 33   *ere ... him:* before ceasing (*left*) to follow him with
LL. 22–3   your gaze.

P. 33 L. 25   *eye-strings:* the muscles or tendons of the eye, believed to break when a man went blind.

P. 34 LL. 8–9   *T'encounter ... him:* Imogen's idea is that when she is at her prayers, her soul is out of her body; if Posthumus prays at the same time, their two souls may meet.

P. 34   *tyrannous ... growing:* like the bitter North wind
LL. 12–13   which brings killing frosts in spring.

P. 34 L. 21   I.5 [1.4]: The conversation between these young gallants is in the affected 'pregnant' style of the times.

crescent note: growing reputation.   P. 34 L. 25

allowed . . . of: acknowledged.   P. 34 L. 26

admiration: amazement; the word had a much   P. 34 L. 27
stronger meaning than today.

makes . . . within: perfect in mind and body.   P. 34 LL. 31-2

words . . . matter: causes him to be slandered.   P. 35 L. 5

approbation . . . quality: the approval of those who   P. 35
sympathize with him for his forced separation from   LL. 7-11
his lady greatly extols (*extends*) his reputation, even
if it be only to support her choice; for had she married a lesser man, her good name would have been
disgraced for choosing a beggar of poor reputation.

creeps acquaintance?: how did he creep into your   P. 35 L. 12
friendship?

will . . . still: however much I repay, I shall always   P. 35 L. 25
be in your debt.

I . . . slight: i.e. I was an inexperienced traveller in   P. 35
those days, and I tended to disagree with (*shunn'd to*   LL. 31-5
go even with) the advice of others rather than to be
guided by their experiences. Nevertheless, upon
further consideration I still hold that it was not an
unimportant matter.

abate her nothing: not allow anything to be taken   P. 36 L. 20
from her reputation.

nor . . . Lady: i.e. the most perfect of all Ladies.   P. 36 LL. 27-8

only . . . Gods: a gift from the gods, and therefore   P. 37 L. 3
not to be sold.

in title: as nominal owner.   P. 37 L. 6

leave here: change the conversation.   P. 37 L. 18

commendation . . . entertainment: letter that I am to be   P. 39 L. 3
made welcome.

lawful counsel: a professional lawyer.   P. 39 L. 13

amplify . . . conclusions: increase my knowledge by   P. 40
other experiments.   LL. 11-12

Allayments . . . act: antidotes.   P. 40 L. 16

quench: put out – let her love die.   P. 41 L. 15

every . . . him: every day makes his condition   P. 41
worse.   LL. 24-5

Thou tak'st: Here the Queen lets fall the supposed   P. 41 L. 28
poison which the Doctor had given her.

P. 42 L. I   *what ... changest on:* i.e. what good fortune will come if you change your loyalty.

P. 42 L. 14   *Leigers:* A leiger was a resident ambassador – for Pisanio is Posthumus's representative at Court.

P. 43 LL. 1–2   *most ... glorious:* i.e. Princesses are most unhappy compared with the lowly.

P. 43 LL. 2–4   *Blessed ... comfort:* how fortunate are humble folk whose desires are satisfied by the produce of the seasons.

P. 43 L. 13   *out of door:* visible, i.e. her beauty.

P. 43 L. 15   *Arabian-Bird:* the Phoenix – used as an image for the rare and beautiful. According to the legend, only one phoenix lived at a time. When it felt death approaching, it made a nest of aromatic twigs which was set alight by the rapid beating of its wings. Out of the ashes a new phoenix was born.

P. 43 L. 18   *Parthian:* The Parthians defeated the heavy-armed and slow-moving Roman legions by their method of fighting. They rode light-armed on swift horses from which they shot arrows into the close ranks, and were away before the Romans could catch them.

P. 43 L. 33   *vaulted arch:* the sky.

P. 44 L. I   *twinn'd stones ... beach:* the innumerable pebbles, all alike, on the sea shore.

P. 44 L. 8   *Contemn with mows:* show their contempt with grimaces. The gist of Iachimo's 'admiration' is that the beauty of Imogen, compared with that of all other women, would move even apes and idiots to excessive wonder.

P. 44 L. 9   *case of favour:* matter of beauty. *favour:* face.

P. 44 LL. 11–13   *Sluttery ... feed:* i.e. even a slut who hates neatness would be disturbed. Iachimo in his feigned ecstasy raves so much that his words lack logic and grammar.

P. 44 LL. 17–18   *Ravening ... garbage:* i.e. the lustful man, always unsatisfied, after devouring the innocent victim goes after filth. These remarks are a prelude to the vile accusation of Posthumus.

P. 44 L. 20   *raps:* makes you enraptured.

P. 44 L. 23   *strange and peevish:* a foreigner and upset.

P. 45 LL. 5–6   *furnaces ... him:* sighs like a furnace.

assured bondage: the bonds of married life. P. 45 L. 12

talents: riches. The talent was the largest sum known P. 45 L. 23
in ancient times.

spur and stop: i.e. keep half-revealing and half-con- P. 46 L. 12
cealing.

Fixing: for the Folio reading *Fiering.* P. 46 L. 18

Slaver . . . common: fouling my lips with the kisses P. 46 L. 19
of harlots.

tomboys . . . yield: harlots hired with the allowance P. 47 LL.4–5
of money (*exhibition*) which you make him.

boil'd stuff: creatures from the hospital for venereal P. 47 L. 7
diseases where the treatment was by sweating baths.

Diana's Priest: Diana was the goddess of chastity. P. 47 L. 17

variable ramps: a succession of whores. P. 47 L. 18

in your despite: in spite of you. P. 47 L. 19

upon your purse: at your expense. P. 47 L. 19

new o'er: a new man. P. 48 L. 15

an . . . chaffless: The worthless chaff was separated P. 48
from the grain by a winnowing-fan. *chaffless:* with- LL. 28–9
out fault.

something curious: somewhat anxious. P. 49 L. 9

outstood my time: i.e. am late in fulfilling my com- P. 49 L. 30
mission.

material . . . present: a matter of importance in offer- P. 49
ing our present to the Emperor. LL. 30–1

kiss'd . . . hit away: In bowls a small ball, called the P. 50 LL. 3–4
jack or *mistress,* is set up as a mark at the end of the
green. From the other end the players propel their
bowls towards the jack; the bowl which finally
rests nearest the jack scores the highest points. A
bowl which actually touches the jack was said to
kiss. An *upcast* is a throw which drives away the op-
ponent's bowl from the jack.

take me up: rebuke. P. 50 L. 6

curtall . . . ears: Cloten uses *curtall* with the sense of P. 50
'cut short' (lit., to cut short the tail of a dog or LL. 13–14
horse). The Second Lord puns on the literal meaning
with *crop the ears,* with a glance at the punishment
given to those who stood in the pillory.

P. 50 L. 17   *smell'd*: with a pun on Cloten's 'rank', which also means 'the coarse scent of a fox'.

P. 50 L. 24   *comb on*: i.e. wearing the cockscomb cap of a professional fool.

P. 51 LL. 12–13 *issues . . . derogate*: don't insult your own children.

P. 51 L. 21   *for his heart*: to save his life.

P. 52 L. 20   *Tarquin*: The story of how Tarquin ravished the chaste Lucrece is told in Shakespeare's *Rape of Lucrece*.

P. 52 L. 21   *rushes*: used as a floor covering.

P. 52 L. 22   *Cytherea*: a title of the goddess Venus.

P. 52 L. 25   *Rubies unparagon'd*: i.e. Imogen's lips. *unparagon'd*: unequalled.

P. 53 L. 1   *arras*: tapestry curtains on which was woven a picture, used in the rooms of the wealthy.

P. 53 L. 8   *Come off*: Here he removes the bracelet which Posthumus had given her at parting (P. 29 L. 12).

P. 53 L. 9   *Gordian-knot*: When Alexander the Great in his conquests reached Gordium he was told that the man who could untie the knot which bound the pole to the yoke of the wagon of King Gordius should be King of Asia. Alexander cut the knot with his sword.

P. 53 L. 20   *Tale of Tereus*: one of the most popular of tales in Shakespeare's time.

P. 54 L. 21   *Mary-buds*: marigolds which close at sundown.

P. 54 L. 26   *horse-hairs and calves'-guts*: fiddle bows and strings.

P. 55 LL. 11–12 *friended . . . season*: make the most of your chances.

P. 55 LL. 16–17   *Save . . . senseless*: except when she orders you to go away and then you pretend not to understand (*are senseless*).

P. 55 L. 19   *So like you*: if it please you.

P. 55 LL. 25–6   *goodness . . . notice*: since he was formerly good to us, we must treat him courteously.

P. 56 L. 2   *Rangers*: foresters, i.e. attendants on Diana the goddess of chastity and the chase.

P. 56 L. 17   *tailors . . . dear*: It was a common jibe of the period that many courtiers owed everything to their smart clothes.

P. 57 L. 1   *say . . . silent*: lest you say that my silence shows assent.

bred of alms: brought up on charity.   P. 57 L. 23

foster'd . . . dishes: fed on the left-overs.   P. 57 L. 23

And though . . . knot: common people – and who P. 57
could be more common than Posthumus – may   LL. 25–8
unite their souls (i.e. marry) but the result will be
nothing more than brats and poverty in a union as
poor as themselves (*self-figur'd knot*).

hilding . . . pantler: a worthless creature (*hilding*) fit P. 57
only to wear a servant's livery, or the household   LL. 32–3
uniform of a squire, or be a pantryman (*pantler*) –
one of the lowest servants in a great household.

preferr'd so well: getting such undeserved promotion. P. 58 L. 6

South-Fog: fogs brought by the South wind were P. 58 L. 7
regarded as pestilential.

Shrew me: bad luck to me.   P. 58 L. 20

make't an action: go to law about it.   P. 58 L. 32

barely gratify: merely repay.   P. 59 L. 16

fresh in their grief: still painful.   P. 59 L. 24

wing-led: in ordered line of battle. Some editors P. 60 L. 1
emend to *mingled*.

Look . . . casement: i.e. like a harlot beckoning to P. 60 L. 16
passers-by.

this stone: i.e. the diamond which was the wager; P. 60 L. 26
see P. 38 L. 26.

brought . . . home: if I had not been intimate with P. 61 LL. 5–6
your mistress.

masterless . . . both: i.e. leave both of us dead. P. 61 L. 16

which . . . spare: i.e. my evidence will be so strong P. 61
that you will need no oath to confirm it.   LL. 21–2

Proud Cleopatra: The meeting of Cleopatra and P. 61 L. 29
Antony on the River Cydnus is gorgeously described in *Antony and Cleopatra*, II.2.

or price: i.e. the value of the riches displayed by P. 61 L. 31
Cleopatra. Sometimes altered to *pride*.

likely . . . themselves: almost able to speak.   P. 62 L. 11

cutter . . . left out: the sculptor surpassed Nature, P. 62
except that his figures could not move or speak.   LL. 11–13

Depending . . . brands: leaning on the logs which they P. 62 L. 21
held up.

P. 62 L. 22   *This . . . honour:* so this is all you can say against her honour!

P. 63 L. 9   *Basilisk:* an imaginary creature with a cock's head, an animal's body, and a snake's tail, hatched out by a toad from a cock's egg – a very deadly beast, able to kill by its mere look.

P. 63 L. 13   *to . . . made:* to the man to whom they swore.

P. 65 L. 1   II.5. There is no division marked in the Folio at this point. The Tirade Misogynous – a denunciation of the faithlessness of women (especially when the speaker is mistaken) – is a common 'set piece' in tragi-comedies. It is later followed by the Protestation Pathetic of injured innocence.

P. 65 L. 3   *to be:* to be procreated.

P. 65 L. 14   *Saturn:* the father of Jupiter, and so the type of extreme old age.

P. 65 L. 17   *yellow:* In the symbolism of colours, yellow signified a variety of unpleasant qualities: here it indicates 'treacheries'.

P. 65 L. 28   *change of Prides:* variety of vanities.

P. 66 L. 4   *true hate:* i.e. the worst one can wish them is that they confound themselves with their evil qualities.

P. 66 L. 33   *ribb'd, and pal'd in:* fenced and enclosed.

P. 67 L. 5   *Came . . . over-came:* Julius Caesar made this famous boast – *veni, vidi, vici* – after his victory over the King of Pontus.

P. 67 L. 13   *Lud's-Town:* London. According to legend (recorded by Holinshed) London was first called Troy-novant (New Troy) but afterwards renamed Lud's Town in honour of King Lud.

P. 67 L. 34   *Mulmutius:* according to Holinshed, the first King of Britain to be crowned with a golden crown, signifying that he was a king and not merely a tribal chief.

P. 68 L. 1   *whose . . . franchise:* i.e. by bringing restitution and freedom.

P. 68 L. 20   *keep at utterance:* preserve by mortal combat.

P. 68 L. 21   *Pannonians and Dalmatians:* tribes living on the Eastern shores of the Adriatic, who rebelled against

the Romans in A.D. 6, and were only subdued after
three years' war.

which . . . read: i.e. to neglect.   P. 68 L. 23

All the remain: so far as you personally are con- P. 68 L. 34
cerned.

locks of counsel: safeguards of secrets – the seals on P. 70 l. 6
letters.

Justice . . . eyes: i.e. the sight of you will compensate P. 70
for all I suffer.   LL. 10–12

mean affairs: humble business.   P. 70 L. 20

bate: abate, i.e. I must restrain my excitement. P. 70 L. 24

thick: fast, all the words running together.   P. 70 L. 26

bores of hearing: ears.   P. 70 L. 27

I . . . through: i.e. I can foresee everything quite P. 71
clearly.   LL. 16–18

Accessible . . . way: the Milford road is the only road P. 71 L. 20
for me.

A . . . ours: i.e. it's too fine for us to stay at home. P. 71 LL. 24–5

gate . . . Heavens: i.e. by having to stoop low P. 71
to enter our cave we learn to bow to the gods.   LL. 25–6

Consider . . . off: reflect that, when from above I P. 72 LL. 3–5
seem to you as small as a crow, the difference
between man and man is just a matter of where each
happens to be standing.

service . . . allowed: i.e. good deeds only count if P. 72 LL. 8–9
they are acknowledged.

attending . . . check: waiting in attendance merely to P. 72 L. 14
be snubbed.

babe: i.e. one who cannot recompense what is done P. 72 L. 15
for him. Sometimes emended to *bauble*.

Prouder . . . uncross'd: i.e. the courtier who rustles so P. 72
finely in his silks gains no more than the obsequious- LL. 16–18
ness of his tailor to whom he owes money.

travailing a bed: travels and labours which are imag- P. 72 L. 26
ined while still in bed.

stride a limit: venture boldly.   P. 72 L. 28

curt'sy . . . censure: receive rebuke with a bow.   P. 73 l. 16

mellow hangings: ripe fruit.   P. 73 L. 24

whereon . . . hit: This is the Folio reading; some- P. 74 L. 14

times emended (perhaps rightly) to 'wherein they bow, their thoughts do hit The roofs etc.'.

P. 74 L. 33   *bar . . . succession:* deprive you of heirs.

P. 75 L. 7   *came from horse:* dismounted.

P. 75 L. 22   *drug-damn'd Italy:* damned for its poisonings. Italians were believed to be capable of any villainy.

P. 75 L. 23   *hard point:* extreme difficulty.

P. 76 L. 15   *False to his bed:* This speech and those that follow form the companion piece to the Tirade Misogynous of II.5; see note on P. 65 L. 1.

P. 76 L. 25   *mother . . . painting:* taught to beautify herself from babyhood.

P. 76 LL. 27–8   *richer . . . ripp'd:* I am too good material to be kept hanging on the walls; like faded tapestry I must be cut up for other uses. Imogen becomes hysterical in her grief and not wholly coherent.

P. 76 L. 29   *men's . . . traitors:* men swear oaths only to betray women.

P. 76 LL. 29–31   *good seeming . . . villainy:* hereafter when a man seems honourable, it will be thought that he is pretending for his own evil purposes.

P. 76 L. 34   *Aeneas:* Aeneas, having escaped from Troy, was kindly entertained by Dido, Queen of Carthage, who fell in love with him. He seduced and deserted her.

P. 76 L. 35   *Sinon:* a Greek who pretended to desert to Troy. He persuaded the Trojans to take into their city the Wooden Horse filled with armed Greeks. When night came, Sinon released his friends from the Horse and Troy fell. He is thus the type of treacherous hypocrite.

P. 77 L. 1   *scandal . . . tear:* cause holy tears to be disregarded.

P. 77 L. 23   *What is here:* Here she takes Posthumus's love-letters from her bosom.

P. 77 L. 33   *fellows:* equals – not commoners like Posthumus.

P. 77 L. 34   *passage:* occurrence – i.e. someday you'll learn the truth of my loyalty.

P. 78 L. 1   *disedg'd:* have taken off the edge of your appetite.

P. 78 L. 19   *unbent:* i.e. unstrung your bow after such preparation for the slaughter of the deer.

elected deer: i.e. chosen victim. P. 78 L. 20

tent: a piece of linen used to probe and cleanse P. 78 L. 28
(*bottom*) a wound.

tread . . . view: i.e. follow a path which would give P. 79
you a full view of what is going on. LL. 33-4

change . . . obedience: become a servant instead of a P. 80 LL. 8-9
Princess.

rarest . . . cheek: i.e. your lovely complexion. Ladies P. 80 L. 14
of rank took great care to keep their skins from sun-
tan.

laboursome . . . trims: the care you took to make your- P. 80 L. 18
self pretty.

made . . . angry: made the Queen of heaven angry. P. 80 L. 19
Juno, wife of Jupiter, was in a state of perpetual (and
natural) jealousy at the amours of her husband.

in their serving: by their help. P. 80 L. 26

happy: lucky, clever – i.e. in singing. P. 80 L. 30

You . . . rich: you have me to keep you richly sup- P. 80 L. 34
plied with money.

from the Queen: see P. 41 L. 28. P. 81 L. 10

sleepy business: which allows us to be slack. P. 82 L. 21

slight in sufferance: easy going. P. 82 L. 30

stand'st so: art so firm in support. P. 83 L. 25

forestall . . . day: i.e. may die during the night. P. 84 L. 6

This paper: the feigned letter sent by Posthumus – P. 85 L. 8
see P. 70 L. 10, and later P. 103 L. 34.

travel: in Shakespeare's time *travel* and *travail* were P. 85 L. 14
the same word.

Foundations: Religious Houses where the poor were P. 87 L. 16
succoured.

lapse in fullness: for a prospering man to lie. P. 87 L. 21

savage hold: stronghold for savages. P. 87 L. 27

Fidele: a three-syllable word, accented Fidéle. P. 89 L. 14

am fallen in: have committed. P. 89 L. 17

well encounter'd: welcome. P. 89 L. 20

Groom in honesty: your honourable bridegroom. P. 89 L. 25

I . . . buy: i.e. I mean business. P. 89 L. 26

Had . . . Posthumus: if these boys had really been my P. 89 L. 33-
brothers then I should have been of as humble birth P. 90 L. 1
as they, and so equal with Posthumus.

P. 90 L. 11   *nothing . . . multitudes:* the worthless flattery of fickle crowds.

P. 91 LL. 3–4   *commands . . . Commission:* gives you supreme powers.

P. 91 L. 21   *saving reverence:* an apology for an improper remark, often abbreviated to 'sirreverence'.

P. 91 L. 22   *fitness . . . fit:* whims come by fits and starts.

P. 91 LL. 28–9   *general services . . . single oppositions:* service in war . . . private quarrels.

P. 91 L. 30   *in my despite:* in spite of me.

P. 91 L. 30   *What . . . is?:* how frail a thing is human life.

P. 92 LL. 17–18   *But clay . . . alike:* living men (*clay and clay*) are of different ranks but in death (*dust*) all men are equal.

P. 92 L. 23   *journal course:* daily custom.

P. 92 L. 29   *Stealing so poorly:* being such a poor chief.

P. 93 L. 10   *meal and bran:* good things and worthless.

P. 93 LL. 11–12   *yet . . . me:* yet I wonder who this 'boy' can be who by some miracle is loved more than I.

P. 93 L. 19   *all's . . . Court:* only courtiers are civilized.

P. 93 LL. 21–3   *Th' imperious . . . fish:* the all-powerful seas produce huge fish, but little rivers fish which are as good for food.

P. 93 L. 25   *stir:* i.e. get his story.

P. 94 L. 20   *stinking elder:* Judas Iscariot according to legend hanged himself on an elder tree which is thus ill-omened. The elder was sometimes used as a support for vines.

P. 94 L. 24   *runagates:* runaways – Pisanio and Imogen.

P. 95 L. 5   *A . . . knock:* I should be a slave if I did not greet such a slave with a blow.

P. 96 L. 14   *lines of favour:* features.

P. 96 LL. 15–16   *snatches . . . speaking:* habit of speaking in spurts.

P. 96 LL. 23–4   *defect . . . fear:* one would naturally expect such a fool to be a coward.

P. 96 L. 33   *perfect what:* I know well enough.

P. 97 L. 1   *take us in:* i.e. as prisoners.

P. 97 LL. 14–15   *honour . . . mutation:* he regarded it as honourable to be perpetually pursuing one object after another. Editors usually emend 'honour' to *humour*.

P. 97 L. 21   *make . . . head:* gather a stronger company.

gain his colour: bring the colour back to his cheeks. P. 98 L. 23

let ... blood: bleed a whole parish. Blood-letting P. 98 L. 24
was a remedy for many sicknesses.

blazon'st: paintest. To blazon is a heraldic term P. 98 L. 28
meaning to paint the coat of arms denoting the noble
ancestry of the bearer.

blowing below: i.e. gently fanning. P. 98 L. 30

give it motion: play it. P. 99 L. 15

toys: trifles – why is he playing a dirge for the boy? P. 99 L. 22

bottom: depth. In former times mariners used to P. 100 L. 4
judge their position by sounding with a lead weight
covered with grease. When raised some of the sea
bottom stuck to the weight, and according to what
was thus revealed the position and the nature of the
anchorage was estimated.

find ... harbour: who could ever find the best place P. 100
in which to bring his dull restlessness (sluggish care) LL. 4–6
to anchor? Some editors ingeniously emend 'care'
to *crare:* a small trading vessel.

but I: I know. P. 100 L. 7

clouted brogues: patched hobnailed shoes. P. 100 L. 17

Fairies ... haunted: i.e. the fairies will keep his body P. 100 L. 21
uncorrupted.

raddock: ruddock, robin. The robin (as in the story P. 100 L. 29
of The Babes in the Wood) is said to bring leaves to
cover the dead.

Thersites ... Aiax: Thersites was the foul-mouthed P. 101 L. 27
jester with the Greek army besieging Troy; Ajax
one of the doughtiest of the Greek warriors.

Mercurial: of Mercury, messenger of the gods, a P. 103 L. 26
pattern of manly beauty.

madded Hecuba: Hecuba was Queen of Troy who P. 103 L. 29
lost all when the Greeks sacked the city. Her lamentable tale was the theme of the Player's speech in
Hamlet (11.2.471–541).

approve: prove the truth of your name – *Fidele:* P. 106 L. 2
faithful.

pickaxes: i.e. fingers. P. 106 L. 11

perform ... loyally: will behave as a loyal subject. P.107 LL.15-16

Now for: if only I had now. P. 107 L. 26

P. 107 L. 27   *amaz'd with matter*: utterly bewildered by events.

P. 107   *Your ... of*: you have forces enough to resist
LL. 29–30   *(affront)* all these that are reported.

P. 107 L. 30   *Come more*: if more come.

P. 107 L. 35   *meet the Time*: face up to our danger.

P. 108 L. 12   *note ... King*: as the King shall see.

P. 108   *This way ... after*: the Romans will either kill us
LL. 23–6   out of hand as Britons or regard us as barbarous and
  unnatural traitors whom they will first make use of
  and afterwards slay.

P. 109 L. 7   *quarter'd fires*: the bivouac fires in their quarters.

P. 109 L. 8   *cloy'd importantly*: filled up with important affairs.

P. 109 L. 9   *our note*: taking notice of us.

P. 109 L. 18   *courtesy ... promis'd*: the royal education which
  your birth expected.

P. 109 L. 19   *Summer's tanlings*: creatures tanned by the sun.

P. 110 L. 17   *am wish'd*: did desire.

P. 111   *To ... within*: i.e. the world assumes that the
LL. 16–17   shabbily dressed man is not so good as the courtier:
  I will show it otherwise.

P. 111 L. 22   *poor soldier*: Posthumus's changes into and out of his
  guise as poor soldier are rapid. Presumably he
  donned a ragged cloak. At P. 112 L. 23 he starts the
  scene as a Briton, but by P. 115 L. 19 he has again
P. 113]   assumed his Roman dress.

LL. 13–14   *run ... base*: play prisoners' base – a boys' game.

P. 113   *faces ... shame*: with faces as fair as – or fairer than –
LL. 15–16   those of young ladies who wear masks to preserve
  their complexions from the weather or to hide their
  blushes of shame.

P. 113 L. 18   *hearts*: with a pun on *harts*: female deer.

P. 113 L. 20   *give you that*: i.e. death.

P. 113 L. 23   *Three ... confident*: as confident as if they had been
  three thousand.

P. 113 L. 24   *file*: i.e. the whole army.

P. 113 L. 28   *distaff*: lit., the staff used by women in spinning – a
  symbol of womanly achievement.

P. 113 L. 28   *gilded*: made red. Shakespeare often uses gold for red.

P. 113 L. 35–   *fly ... eagles*: they run like chickens by the same
–P. 114 L. 1   route that they had swooped *(stoop'd)* like eagles.

slaves . . . made: like slaves they return by the way P. 114
they came as conquerors. LL. 1-2

fragments . . . need: the broken bits of biscuit which P. 114
save the lives of sailors on an over-long voyage. LL. 3-4

mortal bugs: deadly fiends. P. 114 L. 10

vent . . . mock'ry: publish it as a bitter jest. P. 114 L. 16

put . . . rhyme: made me a poet. P. 114 L. 24

Still going: still on the run? This continual criticism P. 114 L. 27
of noblemen and courtiers who are false to the ideals
of their rank is noticeable in this play.

'Tis . . . words: i.e. Death lurks treacherously in the P. 114
soft refinements of a luxurious life but he passes over LL. 34-5
me in battle.

resum'd . . . in: Here he doffs his British soldier's P. 115
garb. LL. 3-4

touch my shoulder: the formal sign of an arrest. P. 115 L. 6

of note: some important person. P. 115 L. 25

penitent instrument: true penitence. P. 116 L. 10

light . . . sake: light coins are accepted at face value. P. 116 L. 25

Thunder-Master: Jupiter, king of the gods. P. 117 L. 4

Mortal Flies: men who die like flies. P. 117 L. 5

stiller seats: i.e. the realms of the dead. P. 118 L. 5

Tenantius: father of Cymbeline; see P. 26 L. 8. P. 118 L. 9

Jupiter descends: In the plays of the 1580s and 1590s P. 118 L. 27
there are several notes for introducing gods and goddesses from 'above' by means of a pulley. This
primitive kind of ingenuity had by now gone
out of fashion and Shakespeare does not use it
elsewhere.

garment . . . covers: i.e. a book which has a better P. 120
cover than contents. LL. 4-5

When as: this cryptic prophecy is later interpreted P. 120
at P. 137 L. 24. LL. 9-15

tongue, and brain not: speak but without under- P. 120 L. 17
standing.

sympathy: resemblance; i.e. this writing is as mud- P. 120 L. 21
dled as my life has been.

death: Death is usually pictured as a skeleton with P. 121 L. 15
an eyeless socket.

jump the after-enquiry: risk the judgement to come. P. 121 LL. 18-19

P. 122 L. 8   *wish . . . in't:* I will wish for a better job for myself.

P. 122 L. 18   *targes of proof:* shields tested for impenetrability.

P. 122 L. 30   *heir . . . reward:* i.e. I shall have to keep the reward which I had hoped to give away.

P. 122 L. 31   *liver . . . brain:* the three vital organs, supposed to be the seats of courage, affection, and intelligence.

P. 123 L. 11   *look like Romans:* i.e. downcast.

P. 123 L. 34   *bore in hand:* pretended.

P. 124 L. 28   *prove . . . feeling:* you have been made to prove my folly by your sufferings.

P. 125 L. 11   *peculiar care:* personal trouble.

P. 128 LL. 5–6 *laming . . . Venus:* making Venus limp.

P. 128 L. 6   *straight-pight:* lit. pitched upright, most dignified.

P. 128 L. 8   *shop . . . qualities:* a place where every kind of quality is stored.

P. 128 L. 9   *hook of wiving:* beauty which allures a man to marry.

P. 128   *which . . . sots:* which was so excellent, when one
LL. 18–21   thought about it, that it showed either that we had boasted (*cracked*) about mere sluts, or else he was so much better in describing beauty that we appeared like fools in our lack of skill.

P. 128 L. 24   *Dian . . . dreams:* as if the goddess of chastity had lustful dreams.

P. 128 L. 29   *In suit:* by asking for it.

P. 128   *carbuncle . . . wheel:* a jewel from the chariot of the
LL. 33–4   sun-god.

P. 129 L. 17   *forfeit:* i.e. her honour.

P. 130   *Peace . . . this:* Imogen is so excited that she cries
LL. 3–4   'hear hear'. To Posthumus she thus appears to be applauding a piece of skilful acting, which moves him to strike her down indignantly.

P. 131   *Why . . . again:* a difficult and much discussed
LL. 11–14 phrase. Imogen means 'Now that you know me, embrace me again, and see whether you still wish to cast me from you.' Several explanations, all rather far-fetched, have been offered, the most popular being that 'rock' is a misprint for *lock:* a throw in wrestling.

P. 131 L. 18   *dullard:* i.e. an actor who has forgotten his part and cannot speak.

undo . . . for: the services you have done me which   P. 133 L. 1
I have not yet rewarded.

on's: of us. The Folio reads *one's.*   P. 133 L. 7

Your . . . offence: my only offence was that you were   P. 134 L. 2
angry.

Their . . . them: because I knew you would feel   P. 134
their loss greatly, the more was I moved (*shaped*) to   LL. 13–15
steal them.

sanguine star: red birthmark.   P. 134 L. 35

starting . . . orbs: leaving the natural course. The   P. 135 L. 9
image is of a planet which leaves its normal motion.

This . . . rich in: this wild summary of your ad-   P. 135
ventures has many details, all of which must be told   LL. 24–6
to make the tale complete.

motives . . . Battle: reasons which brought you to   P. 135 L. 30
the battle.

interrogatories: (pronounced 'intergatories') ques-   P. 135 L. 34
tions to be answered on oath.

so: the Folio reads *no.*   P. 136 L. 14

sprightly shows: supernatural visions.   P. 137 L. 8

Leonatus: 'leo-natus' – lion-born.   P. 137 L. 24

GLOSSARY

absolute: certain

abus'd: wasted

accidents: occurrences

accommodated: assisted

ace: one – the lowest throw in dice

acquittance: discharge of a debt

admiration: excessive emotion, usually of wonder

affected: desired

affiance: loyalty

amend: make better

andirons: firedogs

ape: imitator, idiot

approvers: those who try their worth

attend: wait, wait on

avoid: be off

bane: destruction

bare: make bare, cause to open

barr'd: thwarted

bauble: toy, trifle

bear down: subdue

beastly: mere animals

bent: inclination

big of: pregnant with

bolt: arrow

bond: obligation

boot: addition

brawns: muscles

Britain: Briton

Britany: Britain

Cambria: Wales

car: chariot

carl: churl, peasant

casual: a matter of chance

century: a hundred

chalic'd: cup-like

chance: happening

character: letter, handwriting, fancy shapes

charge: overcome

charm'd: having a charmed life

charms: bewitches

chimney-piece: carving on a mantel piece

cinque-spotted: having five spots

citizen: effeminate

civil: civilized

clipp'd: embraced

close: secretive

clot-pole: blockhead

cloys: claws, rubs the beak on the claws

cock: fighting cock

cognizance: badge, sign

collection: sense

colour: reason

colted: mounted

companion: low fellow

company: body of followers, companions

comparative for: corresponding to

conceited: full of fanciful expressions

conceive: think

conceiving: imagination

conduct: escort

confection: compound

confiners: inhabitants

construction: interpretation

consummation: end

contract: legal marriage

convince: overcome

cordial: effective remedy

corporal: bodily

counter: used in making calculations

cravens: makes cowardly

crook'd: hooked

cross: thwart

curious: elaborately embroidered

deep: weighty

depend: remain

desmesnes: domains, territory

desperate: without hope of recovery

despite: spite

dissembling: deceiving, treacherous

distemper: sickness

donation: gift

doom'd: judged, sentenced

doublet: short coat

dram: lit. one-sixteenth of an ounce

dress: prepare for dinner

earnest: pledge of favours or payments to come

eglantine: sweetbriar

election: choice

Elyzium: place of rest of good spirits

empery: empire

enchaf'd: irritated

enlargement: liberty

entertain: employ

exorcizer: one who calls up the spirits of the dead

even: keep level with

event: sequel, that which happens next

fact: deed

factor: agent

fanes: temples

fangled: fantastic

favour: face, beauty

feat: dextrous

fell: fierce

fit: used in an obscene sense

fitted: made ready

foedary: confederacy

foot: seize with the claws

forbear: depart

fore-end: first part

forfeitor: one who seals a bond and breaks his promise to repay

forfend: forbid

franklin: farmer

fraught: burden

fretted: carved

friend: lover

fumes: vapours

geek: geck, fool

gentle: of gentle birth

giglet: wanton

golden: rich

great: broad, full

gyves: fetters

habit: dress

hand-fast: troth-plight

haply: perhaps

happy: lucky

hardiment: courageous action

hearing: story

herblets: little flowers

hind: peasant
hint: occasion
hold: stronghold
holp: helped
home: thoroughly, entirely
hood-wink'd: blindfolded
hose: breeches
housewife: stay at home
howsoever: nevertheless

imperseverant: stupid
ingenious: cunningly made
injurious: insolent, insulting
intelligence: news
irregulous: knowing no law

Jack-an-apes: monkey
Jarmen: German
jay: harlot
jealousy: suspicion
jet: strut
Jovial: like Jupiter
Juno: wife of Jupiter and Queen of the gods
justicer: judge

ken: view
knowing: intelligence
known: been acquainted

label: writing
'lack: alack
lapp'd: wrapped
lay: bet, pawn
leagu'd: united
leans: is collapsing
learn'd: taught
leaven: that which causes a substance to ferment and go rotten

limb-meal: limb by limb
line: bribe
livers: living people
Lucina: goddess of childbirth
lucre: bribe, desire for gain

Mars: god of war
mart: bargain
match: bet, agreement
meed: reward
mere: utter
mineral: drug, poison
Minerva: goddess of wisdom
minion: darling
minister: work on, be servant to
mo, moe: more
moiety: half share
mother: stepmother
moveable: piece of funiture

neat-herd: cowherd
nice-longing: capricious in their longings
non-pareil: without an equal
note: list

occasions: duties
'Ods-pittikins: by God's pity
o'er-grown: hairy
o'er-laboured: tired out
open'd: revealed
order'd: disciplined
Ord'nance: divine providence
out-craftied: overcome by a subtle trick
out-peer: be superior to
owe: own

packing: making off, conspiring
pain: labour

pandar: one who procures customers for a whore
park: private estate
partition: distinction
partizan: a kind of heavy spear used by palace guards
passable: that which has a way through
perfect: accurately informed
peril: penalty
Phoebus: the sungod
point, at: on the point of
post: travel fast
practise: plot
prefer: cause to be promoted, recommend
pregnant: obvious
presently: immediately
pretence: a plan never intended to be carried out
prevented: forestalled
probation: proof
prone: eager
proof: experience
proper: (a) one's own; (b) handsome
pudency: modesty
puttock: toad

quake: shiver
qualified: full of good qualities

ras'd: erased
rated: valued
rates: scolds
reak: reck, care
reek: steam
referr'd: transferred, married
refts: berefts, takes away by force

religion: scruple
remembrancer: lit. the official who reminds a king of the names of his suitors
render: account
resty: restless
revolt: disloyalty
rowel: point of a spur
runagate: deserter

scruple: doubt
sear up: shrivel
season: age and rank
seconds: helpers
secure: make safe
self-explication: explanation
senseless: insensitive
severally: separately
sharded: with hard shiny wings
shift: change
Sienna: the Duke of Sienna
silly: simple, poor man's
simular: pretended
singular: expert
slip: let go
snuff: smoky candle
sprighted: haunted
spungy: wet
spurs: roots
staggers: giddiness
stale: out of date
stamp: coin
stamped: coined, begotten
stand: stand firm
stand: standing place
stark: stiff
statist: statesman
stew: brothel
still: continuously

stomach-qualm'd: suffering from nausea

stomacher: lit. stomach protector – part of the female costume

stoop: swoop

strain: natural quality

strait: narrow

summer: happy

suppliant: reinforcement

sur-addition: title of honour added to a man's name

sure: faithful

swathing: swaddling

sweet: sweetheart

Synod: Council

table: notebook

tabled: tabulated

talents: riches

temper: mix

tender: offer

tenor: general purpose

tenure: *see* tenor

thorough: through

thrift: profit

throes: labour-pains

through-fare: thoroughfare

tinct: colour

Titan: the sun god

troth: truth

trunk: body

turbonds: turbans

uncivil: barbarous

unfledg'd: still in the nest

unlike: unlikely, extraordinary

unpaved: castrated

untender'd: unoffered, neglected

vantage: opportunity

vassal: servant, subject

vent: give out

virgin-like: white

voucher: guarantee

wage: wager

waggish: impertinent

weeds: garments

wildness: madness

will: lust

windows: eyelids

wink: shut the eyes

winter-ground: cover in winter

work: act

worms: snakes

wrack: wreck

wrings: shows signs of grief

writ: command

wrying: swerving

Zephyr: the gentle west wind